Praise for Sea Fare

When she isn't catching fish on hidden fascinating cultures, like Papua New Guinea, or hanging out with colorful characters, she is serving up the most amazing meals ... and sharing her recipes and secrets. Victoria Allman is as good a writer as she is a cook. I loved reading the book. I wish I could have eaten it.

—Rita Golden Gelman, author of
Tales of a Female Nomad, Living at Large in the World

Acting on wanderlust breeds fantastic discoveries. Making it a lifestyle puts dreams into reality. In *Sea Fare*, Victoria presents a global collage of unscripted culinary experience that offers the reader an honest portrayal in the school of life.

—Chef David Shalleck, author of
Mediterannean Summer

Chef Victoria Allman became hooked on travel following a trip to the Bahamas more than 10 years ago. Since that time she's caught, sautéed, simmered and served her way through the Caribbean, Mediterranean, North America, Europe, Africa, and the South Pacific from Australia to Tahiti. *Sea Fare – a Chef's Journey Across the Ocean* is her travel memoir of food, lust, finding true love and high seas adventure.

—MiamiARTzine

Allman's recipe is equal parts foodie-centric, glamour and adventure, making for a delightful literary repast.

—Seabourn Club Herald

Part memoir, part romance, part travelogue and part cookbook. Anyone who enjoys travel writing and exotic cuisine will love *Sea Fare*.

—The Key West Citizen

Sea Fare serves up a plate full of enthralling stories and delectable recipes giving readers a taste of what it's like to stand in the flip-flops of a megayacht chef, in all of its exotic and harrowing glory.

—The Crew Report

Her story is personally infused with her very human doubts, triumphs and joys. Clearly written, *Sea Fare* includes 30 simple, fresh recipes and while reading it, I felt like I'd taken a trip myself.

—The Urban Coaster

SEAsoned

A Chef's Journey with Her Captain

Victoria Allman

Author of: *Sea Fare*
A Chef's Journey Across the Ocean

Printed in the United States of America

ISBN: 978-1-935254-37-9

Cover Design by NorLightsPress Graphic Department
Book Design by Nadene Carter
Author photo by Suki Finnerty
Illustrations: Dan Brooks graphiccreation@bellsouth.net

First printing, 2011

To Mara and Ella.
There's a great big world out there.
Go explore it.

Contents

Although these stories have all happened to Patrick and me over the past twelve years in yachting, I fictionalized other characters and yachts to protect the extremely guilty.

With Enthusiasm

I'd never seen the ocean turn that particular shade of grey. I could barely tell where the steel grey waves stopped and the concrete grey sky began, especially when the boat heeled to a forty-five-degree angle.

Smash! The starboard cupboard flung open with a force that catapulted half a dozen glass vases from their shelf. They broke apart on the floor like sputtering tomato sauce on a hot stove. I had securely taped that cupboard and thought it was safe, but nothing in my eight years of being a chef on a yacht prepared me for the violence of this storm.

From my refuge on the cool marble floor, I tilted my head and studied the shards of glass scattered in front of me. I thought about pushing myself up off the floor to gather them, but I couldn't summon enough emotion to care. I just wanted to lie there until the storm ended. I turned my head back to the glass aft doors to stare at the horizon, hoping to quell the uneasy feeling in my stomach. Trouble was, I couldn't tell the horizon from the sea.

While searching for that line between sea and sky, I spotted Patrick on deck headed toward the engine room. *What was he doing out there?* I tried to focus. *I should go help him.* I didn't move. *He's your husband.* I lay still. *You love him.* I breathed deeply, still in my fetal position. *He'd help you.* I rolled my eyes, or at least I thought I did. *Damn!*

I finally gathered enough willpower to stand in a crouch and fumble through the main salon. Walking with my knees bent, clutching a couch that was bolted to the floor, I staggered to the back door and watched torrents of water sweep across the teak deck. I counted in my head while a wave rushed over the surface. When it receded, I unlatched the heavy door and scuttled to the engine room hatch. Like the lock of a vault, I grasped the wheel of the door in both hands and twisted, hoping I had the timing right and wouldn't get hit by the next thunderous surge of water.

I stepped through the hole just as the next wave crested. I thrust my whole body into the action of turning the lock. Something clanged inside the mechanism to signal I was safe and dry inside, but as I descended the metal ladder, I didn't feel safe and dry. In fact, I felt as though I'd stepped into the ocean. Water swirled around Patrick as he stood in the engine room, a place best left untouched by salt water.

"What's happening?" I shouted over the roar of the engines.

"I don't know." Patrick's jaw was clenched. The tendons in his neck bulged when he spoke. His blue eyes normally danced like sun on water, but at that moment they were as focused as a bullet.

* * * *

After eight years of working together on yachts, Patrick and I had married six months earlier on the island of Anguilla. The sinking sun lit the path ahead of me as I walked to the water's edge and my future husband. Warm sand squished beneath my feet and stuck between my toes. The hem of my sundress rippled in the breeze. With sea birds soaring overhead as witness, we promised to spend the rest of our lives traveling together.

"In sickness and in health," the official said.

"How about wherever we might find ourselves?" Patrick compromised.

We stood with the Caribbean Sea swishing around our ankles. Patrick stepped closer. He cupped the back of my head with his newly ringed left hand and pulled me in for a kiss. "Are you ready for this adventure?" His voice was a sexy growl.

"I'm ready!"

That was six months earlier, when we chose to stand in ankle-deep water. Now I was having second thoughts about water.

* * * *

"What do you mean, you don't know?" My voice cracked.

His voice was as hard as my knives in the galley and cut just as deep. "I don't know what's wrong! I'm NOT an engineer." This was the first time in our six-month marriage I'd heard him shout.

Why not? I wanted to cry. But I didn't. I understood. We were both over our heads and drowning on this new boat, hopefully just figuratively and not literally.

* * * *

We were used to being at sea. For the past eight years, we'd worked aboard yachts as first mate and chef. We traveled the ocean from the Caribbean up the east coast of Canada, from the Mediterranean to the South Pacific, gaining experiences of life on the water during over a hundred thousand miles of sea voyage. But, those miles were spent on luxurious, prestigious boats that ran with a full crew of qualified professionals; people we trusted, who knew what they were doing. That was before Patrick became the captain of this rapidly sinking ship.

I couldn't blame him. After more than eight years at sea, he had yet to be in charge of his own vessel. He'd supported some of the best captains in the industry and knew how to do it, but he'd never taken the wheel himself.

"I'm getting too old to be a mate again," he told me one day as we sat in a marina bar looking at the line of shiny white hulls reflecting the aquamarine water around them. "I want to look for a captain's job."

I agreed he needed to take the next step. Another job of being mate would be just—another job. He needed to put all his experience, licensing, and knowledge to work. He needed to be a captain.

"We won't be on the kind of boat's you're used to," he warned. "I'll need to start at the bottom and work my way up."

I lifted my margarita to my lips and took a long swallow. I looked out at the gleam of the first polished yacht in the row. Onboard, four crewmembers were outside scrubbing the boat. One held a hose and sprayed fresh water, while another dunked a fuzzy mitt into a bucket of soapy water. While they moved down the length of the passageway, another crewmember followed, scraping away their residue with a blade, like washing the windows of a car. The final body, dressed identically to the others in a navy blue polo and khaki shorts, chamoixed furiously to shine the pristine surface and remove any watermarks left behind. That was what we were used to: attention to detail and an overabundance of bodies to create that prestigious effect.

I had come from galleys that housed induction stoves and indoor grills. Galleys where I had cupboards full of every imaginable shape of dessert mold, shelves of six different flours, and a dizzying array of grades of chocolate for me to choose from. We had a gym onboard and enough space for a desk in our cabin, along with our own flat screen television and DVD player. I was used to luxury, even if I was only the crew onboard.

I told myself it was the tang of the lime in my drink or the punch of the tequila that made me stutter as I spoke. "I know. I don't need all that." *Did I?*

I tried to convince myself I could live without a walk-in fridge and freezer; that I didn't need all that closet space, and the ability to use the yacht's Jacuzzi was an indulgence I wouldn't miss. I loved Patrick. I wanted to support him. I could survive without fourteen other crewmembers to share the workload. I could learn to tie knots and drive tenders. I could perform more than just the duties of chef. I'd been living on a boat for the last eight years. I must have learned something during that time.

* * * *

Yet, there we were, staring at each other, wondering why the sea was rising over our ankles in the engine room. I must admit, my love and support faltered.

"Go up and help Tom," Patrick commanded. "I'll deal with this."

I opened my mouth to reply, but Patrick pointed toward the hatch. "Go!" he said with such adamancy that I dared not say anything more. I turned, climbed the ladder, leaned into the wheel, and opened the hatch a crack, listening and watching for the rush of water. When I deemed my coast clear, I scurried back across the wet deck and through the aft door.

I screwed my face into a mimic. "Go!" I imitated, shaking my head back and forth like a bobble-headed doll. "I can do it," I said like a two-year old. I wanted to be mad, but my insides were still fluttering like a hummingbird's wings. I cross-stepped my way along the main salon, taking a wide berth around the broken glass, and hurried up the stairs to the pilothouse where Tom, our deckhand stood at the wheel, white-knuckled and looking a little green.

"You know we're on autopilot, right?" I asked. His position at the wheel wasn't necessary.

"I know." He didn't move. "I just feel a little more in control here than sitting on the bench." His South African accent faltered when he spoke.

"It's okay, we'll be out of this storm soon." I hoped I sounded more confident than I felt. "This is nothing. We've seen a lot worse." I wanted Tom to have confidence in Patrick. This was his first trip on the boat, after all. Hell, this was our first trip too.

* * * *

Patrick had been captain of this one-hundred-ten-foot boat for only two weeks, and he was exactly right about having to drop down and work his way back up. This craft was less than half the size of the last boat we'd worked on. He took over this vessel from the departing crew in the shipyard, where the sum of their parting words added up to: "Good luck." That should have been our first clue.

In the ensuing days, Patrick crawled through the bilges, sorted through the charts, checked over the safety equipment, and hired our crew: Tom, the deckhand, who had been on one other boat for a single season and Katie, his girlfriend, who had never set foot on anything bigger than a kayak. They weren't our first choice, but time dictated a speedy selection.

Gone were the multiple engineers, qualified stewardesses, and deck crew with experience and sea miles. In their places were two eager crew members with smiling faces.

Patrick felt he had enough experience to teach Tom everything he needed to know, and since I wouldn't be cooking for the fourteen crew and twelve guests I was used to, I would have time to help Katie make beds and dust the blinds every day. We had the knowledge to share, but not the time. We'd barely shown the couple to their bunk and had our first get-to-know each other meeting when the management office called Patrick to tell him they'd booked our first charter.

Katie and I were sitting at the crew mess table as I taught her to fold napkins. Tom was standing in the tiny galley just to our right, grabbing a bottle of water.

"Say your good-bye's to Fort Lauderdale." Patrick's face broke into the bright smile that made him look more like a boy in his twenties than a man in his forties. "We're island bound!"

"Really?" Katie squealed and clasped her hands together.

"Woo hoo!" Tom pumped his fist in the air.

Their excitement was contagious. I smiled and shook my head, remembering the excitement of my first trip to the Bahamas. These guys were in for the time of their lives.

* * * *

All that naivety and excitement seemed far away now.

"Where's Katie?" I asked.

"In the cabin." Tom's wide eyes didn't leave the oncoming waves breaking over the bow. I grabbed at the tabletop as I bounced into a corner from the force of the last drop. Tom's voice didn't skip a beat or even register the shock of the wave. "She's not feeling well."

I wish I could have laughed at his calm understatement. My heart went out to her; the kid was just following her boyfriend, after all. In a way, so was I. She didn't deserve this. The boat careened off the face of another wave and came down hard, shuddering and sending something on the counter of the galley flying. I heard it bounce down the stairs to the crew cabins below. I hoped Katie would have the sense to leave it where it lay and stay in bed. I knew how she felt and wouldn't wish that on anyone.

Crack! I heard the back door slam and breathed a little easier knowing Patrick had returned to relative safety inside the boat. I just hoped the sound I heard wasn't the door breaking open.

"Is everything okay?" I didn't want to ask anything more in front of Tom. I didn't want him to panic about the water in the engine room—at least not yet.

Patrick gave a curt nod of his head. "It's dry down there." He clenched his hands on either side of the radar and stared at the screen. I knew this meant *don't ask any more questions*. In times of stress, I tended to babble, while Patrick reverts to a bare minimum of spoken words. I trusted him. If he said all was okay, then it was. I didn't know how, but he must have fixed the problem.

"How much farther until we're out of the Gulf Stream?"

Tom lit up like a lighthouse through the fog. "Twelve miles until we're on the banks." He'd been paying attention to what Patrick taught him, and he knew the waters would calm over the banks.

"Good." Patrick continued to hold vigilance over the radar screen and the window in front of him. "Hang on, we can make it."

No Calm After the Storm

We stayed glued to our spots for the next twenty minutes. I sat on the couch and curled my legs to my chest, hugging them for comfort and support. The boat rode up the waves and plunged down in jagged intervals. Everything on board was getting a good shaking: including my stomach. Tom sat rigid beside me. His eyes drooped with exhaustion, only to be flung open as we freefell off the next wave.

Patrick stood at the helm, bracing himself against every drop. The radar screen in front of him glowed lime green. A band of neon swept round its face like the second hand of a watch. The night was black around us. The only light in the room was the glow of the screen informing us of islands in the distance. Patrick alternated between staring straight ahead and scanning the distance with the binoculars. There wasn't a mast light to be seen. We were alone.

Whompf! There was a noise like a propane barbecue lighting. The radar in front of Patrick clicked off. The GPS was blank. The navigation system died.

"Shit." Patrick hit the side of the monitor, like any good engineer would do.

I held my breath. He punched at the buttons on the right-hand side of the screen. Nothing happened. He moved over to the twin radar on the other side. It was blank as well. He repeated the action of punching at the keys. Nothing.

"Shit."

I hesitated. I knew I shouldn't ask. I couldn't help myself. "What's happening?"

"We lost all our navigational instruments." Patrick voice was flat.

I rolled my eyes in the dark. *He really must think I'm an idiot.* But, I kept quiet. Tom kept quiet. The minutes ticked by in the dark.

"Shit," Patrick said again.

It was eerie black in that small space. Without the glow of the radar or the light of a full moon, I felt lost and disoriented. I knew I was staring straight ahead out the windows because that's how the chair faced, but I had no other indication of what was around me. The temperature in my body rose and my throat began to close. I giggled a nervous laugh that came out shaky. *Don't panic. Stay calm.*

Whompf! The same sound reverberated through the silence. Once again, the room glowed green. I let out the breath I didn't know I'd been holding and felt my body shaking uncontrollably. In the dim light, Patrick punched at various screens on the bridge. His brow furrowed and he screwed his lips to one side. He wasn't as relieved with the return of the radars as I was.

Patrick grabbed the flashlight from the clip on the wall and started rummaging through our ditch bag. *That wasn't a good sign.* Patrick pulled out the bottles of water I'd packed, the granola bars, and the flares. In his hand, he held the small GPS we would use in an emergency if we had to get in a life raft.

"Okay, we've got radars back, but the nav screen is still down, so we'll need time to re-plot with charts and GPS." He sounded calmer than I knew he was. "Tom, why don't you go get some sleep and Victoria and I will stand watch. You can come back up at eight and we'll go from there."

It didn't take much to convince Tom. The weather had made all of us weary and bone-tired. He bade us goodnight and retreated downstairs.

* * * *

We were huddled in the bridge whispering.

"Are you sure you can do this?" Patrick asked me for the tenth time in as many minutes.

"You've told me a dozen times!" My voice broke the secrecy of a whisper and bordered on squeaking. I was tired and exasperated. "I'm not an idiot."

"I just don't want you to be the weak point of the crew," Patrick hissed. The strain of last night's storm and pressure of the new job was getting to both of us.

I walked out of the pilothouse, silently mimicking his words. "I don't want you to be the weak point." I made an all too familiar face I'd used more than once since this voyage started. I was angry he didn't trust me, but really he had every right not to. I was a chef. I could cook a steak. What did I know about handling lines and tying up a boat? That was the first mate's job. But, we didn't have a first mate. We had me. And that was scary enough for me to pay attention when Patrick explained the procedure to me one more time.

The rough seas had calmed when we entered the shelter of the outer Bahamas and stayed relatively flat for our course through them. I hadn't been able to sleep, but I was able to clean up the broken glass and sort through things that had shifted with all the motion. The bilge pumps had kept working through the night and the boat was no longer in danger of sinking. Patrick explained what had happened—something about a pipe to the air conditioning, but it didn't make sense. All the equipment in the engine room sounded the same to me. There were engines and generators and water makers; I was pretty sure I knew what they did, but it got a little fuzzy when he started talking about pistons and shafts and hoses. I was glad it was still dark in the bridge to mask the glazed faraway look in my eyes. We didn't sink. That was all I needed to know.

Just before dawn, I entered the galley and opened a cupboard. Pots that had shifted during the night crashed to the floor, landing on my bare foot.

"Ow," I muttered.

"Are you okay down there?" Patrick shouted from above. The boat wasn't even large enough to hide a muffled comment.

"Yeah, just the pots and pans." I picked the fallen stack off the floor, replacing all but the nine-inch skillet in the cupboard and locking it. I placed the pan on the stove and turned to the refrigerator. I used my body to block any stray containers that would rocket to the floor if they too had moved. The last thing I wanted was to scramble the eggs on the floor instead of in the pan.

It took three times longer than normal for me to make two simple plates of eggs with cheese. It was all my stomach could handle. As we ate, Patrick went over the docking procedure again.

"You'll be on the aft deck. I can't see what's behind me, so you have to use the handheld radio and tell me everything you see." He had a piece of paper in front of him with a diagram of the marina. He used a pencil to illustrate where we would be docking. He was thorough and organized, a visual person. He needed me to see what would happen; to envision it as he had, and to get it right. "If there is a pole here," he circled an area behind his drawing of our boat, "I need you to tell me how far away it is and what angle it is from the stern. I won't be able to see it and need you to describe EXACTLY where it is."

This all seemed ridiculous. This may not have been as state-of-the-art as our last ride, but it was a multi-million-dollar yacht after all. *Shouldn't the driver be able to see where he was going?*

"I'll call everything," I said in a monotone I hoped he would take as a hint. "I'll throw the stern line first, to the dockhand, when you tell me to." I recited the rest of the speech he'd drilled into my head like I was reading off my grocery list. "I'll tell you when I do it. I'll wait until that line is secured on the cleat on the dock and will then wrap my end around the winch and take up the slack. When the line is tight, I'll wrap it in a figure eight around the cleat on the stern of the boat and tie it off, as you showed me." This was becoming ridiculous. Even Patrick was tired of hearing it.

We sat in silence for the next few minutes, watching the sky turn from black to royal blue to lilac to pink. The formerly grey water sparkled with the emerging light. Slight ripples crinkled the surface, like a bed sheet after a good night's sleep. *What was all that drama about?* We'd made it through the storm and navigated successfully through the night. With the breaking dawn, we were just miles from our destination. It all didn't seem that bad now.

The morning light streamed through the pilothouse windows, illuminating our new home. Patrick was unshaven and rumpled from a night in the same clothes he started in the day before. A ball cap held the blond locks off his face, but didn't cover his smile. He hummed a tune I couldn't quite place as he plotted our course on the paper chart. He was doing what he loved. He was happy. I was proud of him and loved him more at that moment than I ever had.

He turned and smiled at me. He walked over and placed a kiss on my lips. It was tender and made me smile.

"Do you want to practice the knots again?" he asked.

And that feeling of contempt washed over my body again like a wave.

* * * *

I had to admit, it wasn't just me that Patrick drilled on the docking procedure. At eight, when Tom and Katie emerged, he ran through the same process of securing the bow with Tom, but only once. Tom listened and nodded. He'd done this before.

"Do you want me on the radio or to use hand signals?" he asked.

Patrick shook his head, "Good question," he praised. "Keep it handy, but I'll be able to see you, so just hold up your fingers to show how far away we are from the boat in front of us."

Patrick turned to Katie. "Are you excited?"

The chestnut brown ponytail tied high on her head bounced like a cheerleader's pompons. "You bet I am." She rocked onto her tiptoes and smiled widely. "What can I do?"

She reminded me of a Jack Russell terrier with the bright eyes and energetic bounce to match. I was surprised she didn't repeat the question twice.

"We're docking the boat starboard side, which means the right side will be against the dock." Patrick was a good teacher. "We'll have the fenders set up beforehand like big bumpers along the boat. It's your job to make sure they're lined up and at the right height with the dock and any poles that might be there." He grabbed a leather u-shaped harness from the seat behind him. "The lines of the fenders will be on these hooks. Don't be afraid to slide them along the rail to position the fenders where you want them." He turned the hook over and held it out to Katie. "It's lined with fur so it won't scratch or do any damage."

Katie nodded, her ponytail whipping into action again.

"Any questions?"

None of us spoke.

"Good." He looked at his chart again. "We're two miles from the entrance to the port. We'll be on channel thirty-five." He held up the radio to show us the digital display. "Make sure your radio is on and turned up so you can hear me." He thought for a moment. "Let's get this baby tied down and go have some fun."

I thought he was going to make us break a huddle. Tom hurried off to set up the lines and Katie bounded after him to see the view from the aft deck.

Patrick looked at me with concern. "Did I forget anything?"

I leaned over and gave him a kiss on the cheek. "You were perfect."

Patrick looked around to see who was watching. "Not here," he scolded, but with a smile. "Later." He winked at me.

We were in work mode and had agreed not to show affection in front of the crew, so I hurried out of the pilothouse and assumed my position on the aft deck.

* * * *

The day was hot and blinding. While, back home in Canada, it could have been called an autumn day, the air didn't hold a trace of crispness, nor did the foliage look anything but green and tropical. There were no change of seasons in the destinations of this boat. We would perpetually follow summer around the globe.

I lowered my sunglasses and looked over the sparkling water to the white sand beaches along the shoreline. Meringue-like clouds floated in a now baby blue sky. Coconut trees framed the steamy scene. We motored past sherbet-colored gingerbread cottages.

"Are you set up on the aft deck?" Patrick's voice came over the radio on my hip.

I looked at the lines Tom had set up for me, snaked in the exact places Patrick's diagram indicated. The end with a loop on it was threaded through the hole in the back corner of the deck and hung on the rail for me to easily toss to the dockhand. I unclipped the radio, pressed the button on the side, and spoke. "I'm ready back here."

"Are you ready on the bow, Tom?"

There was no answer, but I imagined him giving Patrick the thumbs-up sign.

"I'm ready, too." Katie piped up. She stood not twenty feet away from me at her post. I smiled at her and she beamed back at me. Her big doll-like eyes were hidden behind her glasses, but I knew they sparkled with excitement.

"Okay, guys. I'm going to walk this in slowly. No need to rush."

We were approaching the wooden dock and lining up to slip in between two other yachts—not in a parallel parking way but in a slow sideways nudge. Patrick would nose the boat in, we would throw the lines to shore, and then take up the slack to pull us close.

"Victoria, I want your line on first, then the bow. On my count."

"Roger that," I spoke into the radio and clipped it back on my hip.

"Victoria, how do I look back there?"

I kicked myself. I had forgotten my first job of calling distances to Patrick. I fumbled for the radio. I was about to speak when I realized I couldn't tell how far we were from the other boat. The distance was deceiving. *I'm five feet and I can probably lay down three times between me and their port side,* I surmised. "Fifteen feet to stern." I heard what I was saying as the words came out of my mouth. I hit the button again. "I mean, starboard."

There was silence on the other end of the radio.

I screwed my face into a mental reprimand. I *was* going to be the weak point. I recalculated the distance and spoke again, "Ten feet to starboard and … um…" Shit, I didn't know if I was supposed to call the distance to the tip of the boat's bow or the waterline that angled significantly away from us. "Um, five feet from the tip of the boat."

"Tip of the boat?" Patrick's voice came over the radio. "You mean the bow?"

I don't know. Did I? "Yes, five feet from the bow." We inched even closer to the dock.

"Are we lined up straight to slide in?" Patrick asked.

God, I hope so. "Yes, you look good." *Please be right, please be right.* I pleaded silently with the Boat God.

"Okay, Victoria, throw your line."

I looked down. The thick black rope was splayed out in front of me. Patrick had shown me how to throw it to shore. We stayed late one night, practicing in the parking lot. He demonstrated and made me repeat the action until my shoulder muscles burned like a searing steak. These lines were heavy and awkward and I had never done any sort of arm exercises other than the repetitive chopping of vegetables.

I leaned out over the back railing, holding the line in both hands, and swung the looped end back and forth to gain momentum. It swayed clumsily and struck the side of the boat, sending it askew when I released my grip. I had used my right hand to direct its motion, but it flew off in a shank to the left. It didn't come anywhere close to where the Bahamian boy on the dock waited to catch it. The line struck the water and splashed like an orca at Sea World. *Yikes!* I bent down, picked up the end that was still at my feet, and began pulling the line back, hand over hand. It was heavy enough to begin with, but now it was wet and soggy. I leaned back and used my whole body to reel it in. Drops of water flew everywhere, soaking me and making a mess on the deck. I removed my hand from the line just long enough to wipe the sweat from my forehead. It was hot out there and I missed my air-conditioned galley. My hands smelled like fishy seawater.

I reached over the side of the boat to grab at the loop end and yanked hard to pull enough of the line, now even heavier with water. I quickly re-swung and heaved the line to the boy. I panted with the effort. He, on the other hand, caught the line effortlessly and looped it over the cleat at his feet. He smiled a big toothy grin and gave me a thumbs-up sign before ambling toward the bow to catch Tom's lines. I watched him go, thinking of how laid-back things were here in the Bahamas. No hurry or worry. He wasn't frantic like Patrick and I to make sure the boat docked safely. *What a way to live life.*

"What's happening back there?" Patrick's voice interrupted my thoughts. Once again, I'd forgotten I was supposed to be informing him of every single thing that happened.

I wiped my messy hands on my beige skort and grabbed for my radio. "Stern line is on." I could see Patrick's blond head leaning out over the side of the boat, up forward where the docking station was. He double-checked that I had the right line tied to the dock and nodded. He repeated the double-checking with Tom's line forward.

His voice came over the radio. "Okay, let's start slowly winching ourselves in."

I nodded, knowing he couldn't hear me, but excited that I knew what he wanted me to do. I wound the large black line clockwise around the wheel in the corner and stood up, holding one end in my hands. With my right foot, I stood on the rubber bubble on the deck that started the wheel turning and wound the line tighter. The stern of the boat began moving toward the dock. I held my foot on the button and pulled the slack tight while watching the bow of the yacht behind us to make sure I had given Patrick the right distance and we would slide in without hitting.

"Stop! Stop!" I heard Patrick's voice over the radio as well as shouting from the deck above. I was confused. I looked back at the boat behind me. We were clearing it by five feet. We weren't even close.

"Stop!" Patrick was running down the side of the boat toward me.

I whipped my head around to see what the problem was. We were lined up and ready … but the movement was too fast. We were rapidly approaching the dock. I lifted my foot off the control for the winch and dropped my line.

"Katie, grab that fender!" I yelled and pointed at the same time. I lunged for the other fender that hung on the stern of the boat and tried to move it into place. I unlocked the line it hung on and felt it whirl through my fingers. It was almost in between the corner of the boat and the wooden dock when I heard the first sickening sound. Crunch! Splinters of wood shot straight up in the air as the dock crumbled with the weight of the boat. Crack! One of the boards snapped in two. I stood staring.

Patrick hurtled down the passageway and pushed me out of the way. He bolted past Katie and dove for the fender. I stumbled backward, tripping over the line at my feet. Patrick leaned over the side of the boat, trying to maneuver the fender into place. I thought he was going to flip over the side. He hung from the waist and struggled to push the cushioning into place, but it was too late. The boat came to a grinding halt, half-way into the wooden dock.

We had gone over and over this. He demonstrated every single aspect of the docking. *What had gone wrong?* Never once had he said we would barrel into the dock with such force. He said, 'Loop the line on the cleat and tap your foot on the control to slowly cinch the boat closer to the dock.' My eyes widened in terror. He said 'tap', not 'stand' on the control. Realization washed over me. I had done this. I hadn't listened to the instructions. I had pulled the boat in too fast. I *was* the weak link.

Patrick glare flew wildly from the boat to the dock. He jumped over the side to assess the damage. Deckhands from the boats on either end of us gathered around Patrick. Tom jumped from the boat to the dock to lend a hand. Three Bahamian men in the marina's uniform were coming down the dock to check out what all the commotion was about. Katie and I stayed on the aft—silent.

"Dude, what happened?" A crewmember from the other boat asked.

Patrick's blue eyes turned to steel as he glared at me. He said nothing. He didn't have to. All the guys on the dock looked up at me. Most of them nodded. They knew. I had just screwed up Patrick's first docking.

"Welcome to the Bahamas," I whispered to Katie. "We're here."

The First Impression

*E*verything seemed calmer the next day. The sun shone with a tropical glow. The water around us sparkled with a blue-green luster. We'd moved the boat to a new dock the afternoon before, so there wasn't a constant reminder of the damage I had caused. And most importantly, we'd all slept.

I was up early that morning to prepare for our first set of guests. They would arrive at one o'clock by private plane, and I wanted all my work finished long before then so I could help Katie with the finishing touches of the interior.

We didn't know much about these guests other than two people would arrive, and they wanted to cruise the Exumas. They sent preference sheets through the manager for food requests, so I knew ahead of time what they liked to eat. They had ticked the boxes on the list for light and healthy, no carbs, no desserts, and soymilk. There was an additional hand-written note saying: no oils, dressing, cream, or red meat. Translation, they were health freaks, which was perfect for me. I loved creating fresh, healthy food full of flavor.

The Exumas were remote, with no chance of getting to a grocery store for the next week, so I bought everything ahead in Lauderdale before we left. I studied the preference sheets carefully, making sure I had everything they requested. This new boat was small, with little storage, so I wanted to get it right.

That morning, I prepared a salad with baby French-tipped beans tied in a bundle with chives, heirloom tomatoes, and toasted pine nuts. The vibrant greens and deep reds made it a pretty plate meant to wow. The fresh, clean flavors were to put them at ease and tell them they could trust me and enjoy the food on board. I marinated cod with lemon and thyme for steaming and selected peaches and cherries to be drizzled with amaretto for dessert.

I read through the preference sheets once more to make sure I hadn't missed anything. Light and healthy: check. No carbs: check. No dessert, well, it was just fruit and they could say no if they wanted. No oil, no cream, and no red meat. I had it. I wiped the counters and swept and mopped the floor. A big part of being a yacht chef is cleaning and making the galley look like it's never used.

I was about to remove my apron when the rest of the crew began to stir. Patrick came up the stairs first.

"Good morning, Crash." He wore a grin suggesting he thought he should be opening for Seinfeld. I guessed that meant all was forgiven.

I groaned, hoping the nickname wouldn't stick. "I just wanted your first docking to be memorable."

Patrick laughed. "Well, that it was. Let's just hope the bill from the marina doesn't stick in the owner's memory." He poured himself a cup of Oceana coffee from the pot on the counter.

I nodded. It was one thing to cause the accident, but it would be quite another if I got Patrick fired.

"Breakfast?" I offered as way of an apology.

His wide smile answered my rhetorical question. I placed poached eggs on four plates and warmed tortillas in the pan. I had chopped a mango salsa for the fish earlier, but could afford a few spoonfuls for the crew. I scooped the inside of an avocado and mashed it with lime, cumin, and sea salt. I was placing the plates on the table when Tom and Katie came up the stairs from their cabin.

"Good morning." I motioned for them to sit and eat. "How did you sleep?"

"Much better than the night before," Katie said. "I like being tied to the dock."

Patrick opened his mouth to speak, but I cut him off before he made any comments about parking the boat *inside* the dock.

"After breakfast, I'll help you vacuum and dust," I said to Katie. "We'll make cocktails to greet the guests—something rum-based to welcome them to the Bahamas."

——— VICTORIA ALLMAN ———

"Great!"

* * * *

The morning zoomed by, and soon lunchtime arrived. We changed into our white uniforms and waited for the guests to arrive. Patrick arranged for a car service to pick them up at the airport and had gone to meet them. Tom was on the dock, standing at military ease to help with luggage, while Katie and I lined up on the aft deck holding the trays of refreshment.

"What are these called again?" Katie stared at the tall crystal glasses balanced precariously on her tray.

"Strawberry rum sliders," I said as I watched a long white limo approach the dock. I balanced my tray of hors d'oeurves on one arm and raised the other to my brow to shield the sun piercing through the sky. I squinted, trying to catch the first glimpse of the people we would be catering to for the next week. Patrick jumped out of the car and held the door. One toned and tanned leg swung out gracefully. The woman wore six-inch heels with a satin ribbon winding up her calf like a vine. She held out her hand for Patrick to help her from the limo. A svelte figure in a lemon meringue pie-colored sundress floated out of the back seat. The brim of her straw hat was so large it barely made it through the opening. In one smooth motion she removed the hat like a matador swirling his cape for display and slowly shook her shoulder-length blond locks off her shoulders.

Tom's jaw dropped. Patrick just stared.

She turned and was handed a melon-sized dog. The beige and white shitzu had a pink ribbon in its hair like a ponytail and a diamond choker around its neck. The woman cradled it in her arms like a newborn. Behind her, an offensive guard of a man in a tailored, navy blue jacket emerged. His hair was slicked back off his forehead. In one hand he held a half-smoked cigar, with the other he thrust his briefcase at Patrick. He pulled a long draw off the cigar as he loosened his gold-striped tie.

Who were these people?

As they approached the gangway, I nudged Katie forward. She held out her tray and smiled brightly.

"Welcome," she bubbled, holding her tray high. "Would you like a cocktail?"

The woman pushed her Prada sunglasses up, expertly pinning the curls off her face. Her severely plucked right eyebrow raised in an arch as she looked down her nose at the fruity drinks with sliced pineapple garnishing the rim of the glass. She waved a slender hand in Katie's direction as if she were shooing a fly. The weight of a marble-sized diamond rotated to one side on her skeletal finger.

"A white wine spritzer." At the same time, she pushed the dog at Katie. "Baby needs bottled water."

Katie, who wasn't prepared to hold the squirming pup, reached out to grab him. The tray in her hand tipped to the left. She realized the balance was off and over-corrected. The strawberry smoothies swayed from one side of the rims to the other. Katie's eyes went wide. My eyes went wide. I made a lunge for the tray. Just as my hand grabbed hold, one of the tall glasses teetered on the side of the tray and toppled toward the woman.

A wave of pink left the glass and floated through the air. From where I stood, the pink of the drink was highlighted by the baby blue water in the background. The color was further complimented by the delicate yellow of the woman's dress. They really went well together. Once the first glass went over, the other followed.

The woman's mouth dropped open. No words came out. She clamped her jaw shut and pursed her lips tight. Her eyes narrowed to thin slits as she seethed. The dog leaped from Katie's arms and jumped up on his hind legs. His front paws planted in the woman's skirt and his small pink tongue darted in and out, licking at the fruit oozing down the fabric. Her husband let out a loud guffaw and slapped one knee. The muscles in the woman's jaw clenched even tighter as she glared at her husband. Katie burst into tears. Patrick and I stared at each other, dumbfounded.

I apologized profusely and dabbed at the fabric with a cloth soaked in soda water. Patrick offered to pick up the bill for the dress. Katie left to regroup, while Tom hosed off the deck. The whole time the husband chuckled and the dog bounced up and down with excitement. This was not a good beginning to the trip.

* * * *

Once things had settled down, I went to speak to the missus about lunch. She had changed and was on the aft deck, her voice shrill as she spoke into her cell phone.

"And there's not even a resort or spa here," she wailed. "Can you imagine a place without a jewelry store?"

I hoped to soon have her relaxing and enjoying herself over a meal on the sundeck, and maybe even laughing about the incident, but it sounded like she was worked up about more than just the dress. I waited silently near the bar until she noticed me. She snapped her phone shut.

"I have lunch prepared when you're ready."

"We're on diets," the already anorexic-looking wife declared. "We'll have salad with just lemon juice and egg whites."

I nodded, and changed the menu I had spent hours preparing in my mind to accommodate the request. *There goes my creativity.* But, they were the guests and I was there to cook for them.

I couldn't help but roll my eyes at Patrick when I returned to the galley.

"Are we going to get through this?" he asked with hesitation in his voice.

"Sure, it's only five days, right?"

Patrick stared into space. I guessed my statement wasn't convincing enough.

I started separating egg whites and assembling the salad plates. Katie came back in the galley, her eyes rimmed red.

"I'm so sorry." Her voice trembled.

"Hey, don't worry about it," I said. "These things happen."

"I've never served a tray of drinks before." Katie bit the side of her lip. Tears welled above her eyelids. "I didn't think they would do that."

"Normally, they don't." I smiled reassuringly. "Don't worry, lunch is almost ready and then Tom will get them in the water and they'll start enjoying their vacation."

I squeezed the lemon and sprinkled a touch of sea salt over the greens while Katie announced that lunch was served. I tossed the salad and placed it on beige plates lined with a wave pattern. Katie came back from pouring sparkling water at the table.

"Better?" I asked.

She nodded. "Not a drop spilled." She leaned in and giggled. "Even the dog got Evian."

I laughed and shrugged, then demonstrated how to carry the plates without putting her thumb on the rim. I watched the crazy angle she held the plate and corrected the placement of her fingers.

"Perfect! Okay, you take the salads, and I'll follow behind with the egg whites." I thought for a minute. "You can then grab the peppermill and offer to everyone."

She nodded and we headed out of the galley and up the steps to the sundeck where the table was set with white linen, silver sand dollars, and blue blown-glass starfish decorations. Katie and I had spent a good deal of time that morning arranging flowers for the center of the table. White lilies, lavender orchids, and shiny green leaves were to be the center of attention. But, when we arrived at the table the bouquet had been set on the floor in the corner. In its place sat Baby. She cocked her head to one side and looked at me with her reflective black button eyes.

I placed the plates in front of the guests. The man curled over his plate to inspect the meal, amplifying the roundness of his stomach. He picked up his fork and lifted the egg whites. He looked underneath and then at his wife.

"Where's the meat?"

I stared blankly. Meat? His wife had ordered egg whites for both of them. I looked to her for an answer. She studied her French manicure silently. It only took me a moment to recover.

"I'm sorry, I misunderstood. What can I get for you?"

He pushed the plate in front of him away with one hand. Baby strutted over and began sniffing the eggs on the plate. My mouth dropped. Nobody moved to stop him or shoo him away. The husband curled his lip in a snarl. "Steak and fries, a side of béarnaise."

I guess they weren't both on diets. I flew down the stairs to the galley.

"Can you light the barbecue?" I called to Tom as I passed him in the corridor. "Now!" I added.

I pulled the steaks I had bought for the crew from the fridge. We would have to go without. I scrambled quickly to heat the oil for deep-frying. My knife flew through two potatoes to cut matchsticks as I gently, yet with furor, warmed the butter for the sauce.

"Can I do anything?" Katie asked.

"Just stand back and watch the show." I could hear the pride in Patrick's voice. He knew I could handle last minute requests, this wasn't the first one I'd had, but it still didn't make them any easier or welcome.

I thrust the platter with tenderloin into his hands. "You're now my grill guy." I felt like I was back in a restaurant armed with prep-cooks and apprentices. "Cook this medium-rare."

I pivoted on one foot to Katie. "He'll need ketchup and Dijon mustard. The small white china dishes in the dining room will work perfectly." She turned to leave the galley as I called after her, "And a pitcher and ladle for the sauce."

I smiled to myself. Patrick was right: I did enjoy the adrenalin rush of last minute requests.

It wasn't long before I had another whole meal plated and ready to go. Katie carried the plate, and I followed with the sauces.

The wife had Baby in her lap. She was trying to hand-feed the little ball of fur the egg whites from earlier. Her diamond tennis bracelet tinkled against the dish.

She cooed to him with a syrupy singsong voice, "Here you go, little one." She waved the whites in front of his nose. "See what Mama has for you." Baby was having none of it. He turned his wet nose away from the woman.

She shook her head. "This will not do," she said to me. "You will have to make him white fish." She picked up Baby and held him to her face, Eskimo kissing and crooning. "You'd like that, wouldn't you sweetie?"

I bit my tongue so hard the metallic taste of blood filled my mouth. I returned to the galley to start my fourth lunch of the day. This was going to be a *long* week.

Poached Eggs
with Mango Salsa and Avocado

Mango Salsa:
1 ripe mango
1/2 red onion
4 tomatoes
1/4 - 1/2 habanero pepper, depending on heat tolerance
1/4 cup chopped cilantro leaves
2 limes, juiced
1 teaspoon sea salt

Dice the mango and red onion to uniform quarter-inch size. Cut the inner seeds and pulp out of the tomato leaving a flat fillet of tomato to work with. Dice the fillet to a quarter-inch size. Chop the habanero as small as possible to evenly distribute heat. Mix all ingredients together; taste for seasoning.

Avocado Puree:
2 Hass avocados, deseeded and flesh scooped out
1 lime, juiced
1/8 habenero pepper, depending on heat tolerance, minced
1/2 teaspoons sea salt
1/4 tespoon cumin
1/4 cup water

~Continued on next page

In a food processor, puree all ingredients together and pass through a seive. Taste for seasoning.

Poached Eggs:
6 eggs
1.5 gallons water
2 teaspoons sea salt
1 teaspoon white vinegar

Combine water, sea salt and vinegar in a wide heavy saucepan and bring to a simmer.
Break 1 egg into a small bowl or cup and slide egg into water. Repeat with each remaining egg, spacing them evenly in saucepan, and poach at a bare simmer until whites are firm and yolks are still runny, 2 to 3 minutes. Transfer eggs as cooked to a tea towel, to absorb excess water, using a slotted spoon.

Assembly:
Flour Tortillas
Avocado Slices
Tomato Slices
Sea Salt
Poached Eggs
Mango Salsa
Avocado Puree
Cilantro Leaves

Stack seasoned avocado slices and tomato on top of warmed tortillas. Carefully place the poached egg on top and garnish with salsa, avocado puree, and cilantro leaves.

Serves 6

Strawberry Rum Sliders

8 oz coconut Rum
2 limes, juiced
4 teaspoons sugar
24 strawberries
4 bananas
2 cups ice cubes

Wash and hull the strawberries. Pour the rum and squeezed lime juice into a blender with the sugar and let sit one minute. Add the strawberries, banana and ice cubes. Blend for twenty seconds until smooth. Pour into tall glass and garnish with strawberries.

Serve, repeat...possibly multiple times.

Serves 4

The Heart of the Bahamas

*A*fter the guests retired to bed, we moved the boat from the dock to a secluded anchorage. Patrick wanted them to awaken in a beautiful new setting. New place, new start. It took a few hours to cruise there and set the anchor, so the crew was up half the night and again early the next morning. This was exhausting, but would be worth it if we could erase their memory of the day before.

This time, I would be prepared for anything. I sliced a pineapple with mangoes, papaya, and kiwi for her, and also fried strips of applewood smoked bacon for him.

Tom was outside chamoixing the aft deck while Katie cleaned the main salon. So far, this was going well. Mind you, it was only 7:30 in the morning.

The mister thumped down the passageway and into the galley as I was pulling applesauce muffins from the oven. The smell of cinnamon puffed out like a cloud. The sweetness drugged me and I couldn't help but smile.

"Good morning," I chirped. "How did you sleep?"

He raised one droopy eyelid and grumbled. "Coffee. Now."

So much for morning pleasantries. He grabbed the steaming mug from my hands and dumped four heaping spoons of sugar into it. The sound of his spoon hitting the cup rang through the galley. He pulled a muffin out of the tray and shoved the whole thing in his mouth. "What's there to do on this island?" Bits of baked goods sprayed from his mouth as he talked and chewed at the same time.

"The beach is lovely this time of…"

He cut me off with a scowl. "Long walk on the beach with my wife, looking for seashells?" He scoffed as he grabbed four slices of bacon in his meaty hands. "I don't think so. What else ya got?" His accent betrayed more Jersey Shore than Upper East Side.

"Kayaking?" I offered.

He glared.

"The boat has two jet-skis?"

Again, the eyelid raised. "Good." He grabbed three more pieces of bacon and turned to leave. "Get me one ready."

"I'll have Patrick give you a tour of the area." I picked up the intercom.

The man growled, "I don't need a babysitter." He left the galley, but yelled back. "Just get me a ski."

I clenched my jaw and repeated, "Just four more days, just four more days."

Tom walked through the galley as I hung up the phone. "Patrick would like you to take the jet-ski for a spin to make sure it's working before Mister gets on it," I said. "He'll meet you on the bow to help get it in the water."

Tom's eyes lit up. His smile widened. "Great! I'll be right there." He bounded down the stairs to his cabin to change.

Katie trudged into the galley carrying her cleaning caddy. She crinkled her nose and stuck out her tongue. "Ugh! You should see the state of that man's bathroom." She flung herself down on the setee. "It's disgusting."

I smiled sympathetically. I could only imagine, and it made me all the more grateful to be the chef. Sure, I had to get up earlier and work longer hours, but I didn't have to clean other people's toilets.

Tom ran up the stairs, now wearing his water-sports uniform of blue board shorts and a white rash guard with the boat's logo on his left breast. The form-fitting material stretched over his broad chest. The kid had been outside scrubbing the boat for the past month and was developing the tan and muscles to prove it. His Oakley's hung from a cord around his neck. He looked every bit the part of a crewmember in the islands.

"Hey Katie, Patrick needs me to go jet-skiing." He squealed like a kid on Christmas morning. "Isn't this job great!" He bolted out the door as Katie looked down at the toilet brush in her hands.

"Yeah, great," she mumbled as she dragged herself from the table. "If you need me, I'll be in the guest cabin ironing."

I tried to smile supportively, but I knew how Katie felt. I, too, had often felt jilted when Patrick would take the guests diving while I stayed behind to make lunch, or when we pulled into a new port and he headed out to explore, while I went to the grocery store.

Once, after we'd been in Tahiti and come home again, Patrick was telling a friend how every morning he would have his coffee on the bow of the boat and watch the whales in the bay.

"What?" I practically choked on my drink. "I never saw any whales."

"They were there every morning," he scoffed, like I was being silly.

"Where was I?" I couldn't believe this was the first I was hearing of it.

Patrick shrugged. "You were cooking breakfast."

This time, I actually spit my drink as I shouted. "For you! I was making breakfast for you! And you never thought to come get me?"

That was one of those moments where living together twenty-four hours a day in a confined space gets to you. No matter how much you love your partner, at times you want to kill him. I knew what Katie was feeling right now.

"Hey, if the missus goes jet-skiing too, we'll go for a swim." It was the only solace I could offer. Stolen moments of fun can make up for a lot on a boat.

Katie smiled weakly. "If she leaves, then I'm going to take a nap." She blew the bangs out of her eyes. "I'm exhausted."

She slunk out of the galley and down the corridor. I felt for her. Her earlier enthusiasm was deflating like a leaky air mattress.

I tidied up the galley and went to see if the guys needed help on the aft deck.

Patrick stood watching Tom cut a wide figure eight in the flat turquoise water surrounding the boat. "Looks like he's having fun," I said. "Is he doing okay?"

"Yeah, he'll be great." Patrick kept an eye on Tom as he spoke. "He's a natural and is picking everything up quickly." He turned to me. "How's Katie doing?"

"She's okay," I said, not one hundred percent convinced. "She just needs some sleep and a little fun. Last night was rough, but she'll get there."

Patrick nodded and focused his attention on Tom, who was pulling up to the back of the boat. He was coming in fast and straight, a huge grin on his face. Patrick began circling his arms to indicate he should curve wide and come along side. Tom kept to his course. Patrick shouted, "Slow down."

"What?" Tom shouted over the roar of the motor.

Patrick held his hands up and waved them like a third base coach. "Stop!"

Tom began to slow down, but it was too late. The bow of the jet-ski hit the swim platform and rose out of the water with a dull thud. The momentum propelled it further up onto the deck. Tom's smile changed to a look of confusion. Patrick jumped back and pushed me out of the way. Like Shamu beaching himself for applause and a handful of sardines, the jet-ski teetered on the deck for a moment before slowly sliding back into the water, leaving behind a deep scratch in the teak, along with flecks of chipped red paint.

Patrick clenched his jaw so tight I could see the tendons in his neck bulge. He opened his mouth to say something, but shut it again. Tom floated a few feet behind the boat looking dazed.

I got to my feet and called to him. "Are you okay?"

"Yeah, sorry. I didn't think it would do that." He looked at Patrick. "I'm sorry, Captain."

Patrick took a deep breath to compose himself. "No problem. I've done worse." He tried to smile, but wasn't all that convincing. "I'll teach you how to sand the teak, and we can patch the bottom of the ski later."

Patrick and I looked at each other. We would all need to get our acts together if we were going to make this boat work as a successful charter yacht.

* * * *

"Ready?" the man bellowed from the aft deck. He had just emerged from his cabin, wearing baby blue swim shorts with pink paisley swirls. His stomach folded over the waistband and stuck out of the orange and yellow aloha shirt that screamed "tourist trying too hard." He was oblivious to the earlier mishap. Tom had tied the jet-ski off successfully with the second attempt, and we loaded water and a handheld radio into the storage compartment.

I held a lifejacket out for him, but he strode right past it.

"Um, Sir." Patrick grabbed the jacket out of my hand and held it out for the man. "It's law that you wear a PFD."

Like Vanna White, the man waved his hand. "See any cops?"

"Still, I would feel more comfortable…" Patrick began.

The man snatched the preserver out of my hands. "Jeez. Some fun vacation this is." He lifted the lid of the seat, shoved the jacket in, and slammed the lid shut. "There, happy now?"

Patrick smiled through gritted teeth as he reached down to untie the ski from the cleat. He held the line in his hand while the man stepped onboard. It sank low in the water. "See ya." He roared off, ripping the line out of Patrick's hand.

"Watch the line!" Patrick shouted. "It will tangle in the shaft."

The man was already fifty feet away when he cut the engine and reached forward for the line. We watched helplessly as the ski shifted under his weight and like a Bozo Bop Bag, tipped the man off and into the water before popping up again. He splashed headfirst over the handlebars and was instantly submerged in the warm salty water. I couldn't help but laugh.

He came up sputtering and cursing a few feet from the ski. His long, normally slicked back hair hung in his eyes. He clung to the side of the ski and whipped his head around.

"Are you okay?" Patrick shouted across the water.

The man kept searching the water wildly as he struggled to get up on the ski. "What's in the water?" He squealed like a little girl. "Are there sharks in this water?" He spun around in a circle, gyrating like a washing machine. "What was that?"

"Don't panic," Patrick shouted. "You're okay."

The man pulled himself half way up on the ski before it flipped again, sending him back into the ocean. Expletives carried over the water.

"Hang on, I'm coming" Patrick called. He climbed into the tender to perform a daring sea rescue, in fifteen feet of calm idyllic water, one hundred yards from shore. He covered the distance to the man in no time and cut the engine of the dingy. Patrick leaned over the side and grabbed the jet-ski rope in one hand while steadying the ski with the other. With the help of the dingy to hold onto, the man scrambled up and onto the ski, still cursing.

Again, he snatched the rope out of Patrick's hand and sped off, this time with the rope in his hand instead of dangling in the water. I heard no thank you uttered. Just another service we offered.

* * * *

"Lady!" the voice shouted from somewhere outside the galley. "Hey, lady!"

I thought it might be the man returning on his ski. He'd been gone for over an hour. His wife hadn't come out of her cabin yet and, although we were enjoying the quiet, we were starting to wonder where the man had gone. Tom stood guard to help him back onboard, but maybe he'd slipped past unseen. I dried my hands and stepped onto deck. The Bahamian sun sizzled against my skin. I needed to remember to wear sunscreen. I raised a hand to my brow to shield the shimmering light. There was no jet ski in sight, but I peered over the rail to a worn wooden skiff below.

"Good morning," I called to the Bahamian man at the tiller.

"Good mornin', lady. How's you today?" The man smiled a wide toothless grin. His boat was loaded with conch, grouper, and lobster. "Swannee here." He tapped his bare chest. "You need fish?"

This was what I loved about being on a boat. "What have you got?"

"'Dis mornin' I got's you something special." He twisted his upper body to reach behind him. Each bone of his ribcage rippled down his dark skin. His hand-me-down shorts were cinched tight with a length of nylon cord. Bare feet and a Gilligan's hat, frayed at the rim, completed his uniform. Life was simpler here in the islands.

From behind his back, Swannee pulled two slender stalks, looking like thick white asparagus without their heads. He looked at me with all seriousness. His eyes squinted, his voice lowered.

"You ever ate fresh hearts of palm?"

Fresh hearts of palm? Did he mean those soggy, smushy things in a can? I shook my head.

Swannee twisted again on his gnarled, weather-beaten stoop. If he was pricked by the inevitable splinters, he didn't wince. He pointed. Sunlight sparkled off the still water, glittering like sapphires and aquamarines. Over the white-sand beach in the distance stood half a dozen coconut trees curved low over the water.

"I just gots them for you." He held the stalks out for inspection. "They go good with my fish."

I knew hearts of palm were, as the name inferred, the heart of the coconut palm tree, but hadn't ever had one fresh. Swannee pulled a machete from under his seat, and with the palm heart in his left hand; he began shucking the tough outer sheath to get to the delicate inner core. He shaved a thin slice across the diameter, miraculously not cutting into his thumb with the blade, and handed it up to me.

I let the new experience sit on my tongue, feeling the velvety flesh before chewing. It was crunchy with a mild nutty flavor, similar to an artichoke. I loved it. This wasn't the same thing that came out of a can. This was delicate and firm, all at the same time. This vegetable had a soft creamy bite. My mind whirled with the possibilities for salads.

"You like?" Swannee asked.

I looked across the intricate pattern of clear turquoise water, to the steamy tropical beach, and back. "I like." I nodded. "I'll take six lobsters and six hearts."

Swannee smiled wide and threw the lobsters up on deck while I returned to the galley to grab some cash from my drawer.

"That jet-ski belong to dis' boat?" Swannee asked when I returned.

"A red jet-ski?" I asked, afraid of what he was going to say next. No doubt the man was running it like a madman and disturbing the peace of the island.

Swannee nodded. "De one run up in the mangroves on de other side of de island?"

I took a deep breath. "Did you see anyone with it?"

Swannee shook his head. "Nah, I was just cuttin' the hearts and saw de ski." He twisted the throttle on the motor slightly and started off. He turned again on his seat and called over his shoulder, "It don't look too good. All banged up."

I hardly heard his last statement. I turned on my heel and was running for the pilothouse. "PATRICK!"

Applesauce Cinnamon Muffins

1-1/2 cups flour
1 cup brown sugar
1-1/2 teaspoons baking powder
1/2 teaspoon baking soda
1 teaspoon cinnamon
1/4 teaspoon all spice
1 cup raisins
3/4 cup walnuts
2 eggs
1/2 cup melted butter
1 cup applesauce

~Continued on next page

—— *SEAsoned* ——

Pre-heat oven to 350 degrees. Grease muffin pan.

Toast the walnuts on a cookie sheet in the oven for 5 minutes until they begin to release a nutty smell. Cool and chop.

Stir together flour, brown sugar, baking powder, baking soda and spices in a bowl. Add raisins and walnuts and stir to coat with flour. Whisk together eggs, butter and applesauce in a separate bowl until combined well. Fold liquid mixture into flour mixture until flour is just moistened. Do not over mix. Divide batter among twelve muffin cups.

Bake until muffins are puffed and golden, about 20 minutes. Cool slightly.

Makes 12 muffins

Fresh Hearts of Palm Salad

6-six-inch stalks hearts of palm (or 1-14 oz can)
1 shallot, minced
1/4 cup Italian parsley, chopped fine
1 lemon, juiced
1/2 teaspoon Dijon mustard
1/2 teaspoon sea salt
1/2 teaspoon sugar
1/8 teaspoon black pepper
1/4 cup extra-virgin olive oil

Using a Japanese mandoline, slice the hearts of palm thinly into matchsticks. Whisk together shallot, parsley, lemon juice, Dijon mustard, sea salt, sugar and black pepper. Slowly drizzle in olive oil, whisking constantly until oil is incorporated. Toss the vinaigrette with the hearts of palm and serve.

Serve as a small salad, or as a side with fish or chicken.

Serves 4

Search and Rescue

"Shhh," Patrick hissed as I came crashing into the pilothouse. "You'll wake the dragon lady." He started to laugh, but caught the look on my face. "What? What's happened?"

"A local fisherman was just here and said he saw the ski stuck in the mangroves."

"Shit." I rarely heard Patrick swear, but he was becoming quite good at it on this boat. "Was our guy with it?"

I shook my head.

"Shit." Patrick slammed the logbook shut and bolted from the room. I followed.

Tom was polishing the back rails when we got to the aft deck. "Victoria and I are going to look for the jet-ski. I need you to stay on board and keep an eye on things. Watch the GPS to make sure we're not dragging anchor." He reached down to pull the tender close. "And stick your head in the engine room every now and then to check the generator."

Tom's chest swelled with pride at the responsibility.

"Missus isn't up yet," I added. "You and Katie will have to deal with her if she comes out." Tom's face fell. "I'll be back to make breakfast for her soon."

Patrick started the engine and Tom untied the line. Salty spray misted my skin as we hovered over the water. Patrick curved wide and circled the island to the south. In the far distance, we saw sailboats anchored and the dock of the island yacht club. I assumed that was where the man had gone. But, between us and the marina was a row of mangroves. Their roots bridged over the water in a tangle of veins from the main trunk. They lined the shore like an impenetrable fence, providing a safe home for fish to dart in and out, and a strainer for garbage floating in the water. A plastic bag wrapped around one of the roots and a plastic coke bottle stuck in the mesh. I shook my head. Even out here, paradise was being ruined by thoughtlessness.

I scanned the line of shrubs for the ski. Half way down, I saw it. Swannee was right. It was sandwiched between two trees, hanging high on the bow with the back submerged. Branches were snapped all around and there was a long, deep scratch down the side.

I looked left and right. No sign of the man. Patrick pulled up to the ski, scanning the water and the grove at the same time. "There's no way he got through there without breaking his ankle." Patrick looked around again. "And he wouldn't fit through the branches."

"The yacht club?" I wondered if he would have swum that far.

Patrick clenched his jaw and motored off toward the dock. His silence was not a good sign.

We wove through the moored sailboats to the wooden dock. The boats were thirty- to forty-foot cruisers occupied by live-aboard sailors, who spent the winters hopping from island to island, slowly making their way down the chain and exploring each place thoroughly. We ran into them everywhere in the Bahamas, and I was always intrigued by their lifestyle. Typically, they were husband and wife teams who traveled from place to place with no set schedule and no set obligations. If they felt like sleeping in, they slept in. If they felt like eating, they ate. Their only responsibility in life was to maintain the boat. In the tropical sun, surrounded by blue, this seemed idyllic to me. I waved hello to a woman who was topside, hanging her laundry to dry in the Bahamian breeze. She wasn't off chasing some crazy guest, responsible for whatever trouble he got in. Her only concern for the day was whether to grill fresh-caught fish for lunch or save it for dinner. I sighed.

I steadied the tender as Patrick jumped out and headed up the conch-shell-lined path to the main house. I tied off the line and hurried after him.

"Well, it's about time you got here," the man's voice bellowed from inside.

——— Victoria Allman ———

I stepped through the screen door to an L-shaped tiki bar. Rough-hewn wooden timbers were exposed and plastered with life rings from various boats. Blue and green glass balls wrapped in cord hung from the rafters. An old ship's wheel was mounted behind the bar and surrounded by bottles of rum from the islands.

Mister was sitting on a high barstool surrounded by three Bahamian fishermen. He had a highball in his hand and two empty glasses in front of him. "I was just telling Wes here how I needed to get back to my yacht."

The bartender rolled his eyes and removed the empties. "Yeah, he's been tellin' us all about his big boat."

Patrick unclenched his jaw long enough to ask, "What happened?"

Mister swiveled in his chair to look at Patrick. "I needed to take a leak, so I headed to shore." He slapped the man beside him on his back. "That's when these guys pulled up and brought me here for a drink." He rattled the ice in his glass at the bartender. "Another."

"And the ski?" Patrick asked.

The man waved his hand. "It's out there. You can pick it up." He turned his back to Patrick and downed the rum. He slammed the glass back on the bar. "Let's go."

Mister stormed out the door, letting it slam behind him. Patrick and I stood there speechless. One of the Bahamians laughed, shaking his head, "Dat man, is gonna gets himself killed on dat ting." Patrick nodded. "He ran it so fast and hard up in dem trees I's surprised he didn't lose his head."

"Thanks for getting him," I said.

"Dat no problem," the man beamed wide. "He buys us all drinks."

Patrick laughed for the first time that morning.

The bartender flung his white bar towel over his shoulder. "Dat will be one hundred and eighty-six dollars."

Patrick stopped laughing. "Of course." He shook his head and reached for his wallet. A captain's responsibility covers a lot of things. "There's another hundred on the tab if you guys help my deckhand get the ski out."

The fishermen nodded. "No worries man."

"Okay, thanks." Patrick turned to leave.

"Good luck with dat one." The bartender nodded his head toward our guest. "He's a mean one."

* * * *

Back on board, Mister went straight to the sundeck to lie on a chaise and read. "I'll have eggs Benedict and a bloody Mary."

Eggs Benedict? I looked at my watch. It felt like I'd been up for hours, but it was still early, only ten in the morning. I headed to the galley to start whisking the sauce.

* * * *

"Good Morning." The Missus appearance in the galley startled me, not to mention her pleasant tone of voice. "We have guests arriving at one. We're going to swim and eat lunch on the sundeck."

I smiled my *I'm-talking-to-the-guests smile*. "Wonderful, how many people?" I wondered who would be friends with these people and where they would come from.

"There's us and eight on *Sunchaser*. So, that's ten." The smile stayed plastered on my face, hers skewed to one side in question. "I'm not sure how many are coming from *Wave Rider* though."

I felt like the Joker, a fake grin painted on my skin. Guests arriving from two different yachts could get ugly. We weren't prepared for this. Tom was still out with the jet-ski and Katie was rattled from the night before. I had lunch started, but only for two. I needed to get moving and quick. It wasn't that early and I had a lot of prep to do for ten, or more, people.

"Do you have anything in mind?" My mind raced. I planned to serve the lobster tails from Swannee with a corn salad and the hearts of palm. But, I didn't have enough for everyone. I could grill rib-eyes and chicken to increase the volume. A barbecue would be perfect at anchor under the tropical sun. I had heirloom tomatoes for a salsa and romaine I could toss into a salad. "Perhaps a barbecue?" I hoped she couldn't hear the rising panic in my voice.

"Mmm, that would work." Missus nodded her head. "But, something fancy. Nothing ordinary." She lingered. She picked up a magazine and flipped through the pages. "I don't want anything fattening."

I expanded my smile, but didn't say a word. *My mind raced. Did I have enough limes to make a ceviche? Could I bake a chocolate chiffon cake in time?*

Finally, missus wandered beyond the galley doors, and I was free to whirl around the galley. I pulled meats and vegetables from the fridge. I placed a pot of water on the stove to boil and started shucking ears of corn. I sliced cherry tomatoes and diced red onions. I felt my brow furrow. I concentrated while my knife struck the cutting board like a woodpecker.

Patrick came in and backed out again when he saw the pace at which I was moving. He knew me well enough to know this wasn't a good time to talk.

I melted chocolate slowly over simmering water while whipping egg whites furiously for the cake. I rinsed strawberries to marinate in Grand Marnier for ice cream.

The grinding of the mechanics in the galley door signaled Missus' return. "Did I tell you our friend Alex is a vegetarian?" She flashed through the galley like lightning.

I didn't have time to soak and cook black beans for a burger. I hoped she would be satisfied with ones I had previously frozen for just such an occurrence. She would have to be. I cursed silently, knowing how much better the meal would be if I'd known some of this the night before.

Katie stuck her head in the door. "Do you want the table set, or a buffet?" We'd gone over each scenario previously.

"Buffet," I said, not even looking up from my cutting board. She retreated, and I continued to whirl.

When Missus next returned to the galley I was half way through mashing avocados for guacamole. The smile had returned to my face. "They should be here any minute," she said. "We'll have a fruit platter and some of those muffins you baked." It was not a question. "I'm not sure if they've had breakfast yet." She breezed in so fast she made the request sound as easy as a wave of the wand.

"Of course." I clenched my fist tight around the chef's knife and slammed it down on the cutting board, scraping it across the surface and scooping the avocado skins into the garbage. I spun on my heel to grab two mixing bowls for the muffin batter. The ones from this morning had all been scarfed by her husband. They needed twenty minutes in the oven. *Would they be ready in time?*

I bathed and spun lettuce. I toasted pine nuts and shaved Parmesan to decorate the salad. My forearm ached when I whisked olive oil into sherry vinegar and Dijon for a dressing.

I checked the clock. Ten minutes to one. Katie darted in and out, trying to set the table and get drinks at the same time.

"Just mix jugs of iced tea and margaritas for the bar on the sundeck," I told her. "That way you can pour up there and not use a tray."

She looked relieved. "Great idea. Thanks." She bolted from the galley and up the steps.

I looked around the galley. The salads were prepared, the meats were ready to grill. Dessert was all but plated. I placed the last of the sliced pineapple on the platter. I was ready. I smiled to myself. Bring it on.

Missus came through the door again. She was dressed in a sheer beaded cover-up. Her hair, pulled back in an elegant ponytail, revealed more diamonds dangling from her ears. She was beautiful. "There's been a change of plans." She barely broke stride. "Have the captain get the tender ready." She sailed out of the galley calling over her shoulder, "We've been invited to *Sunchaser* for lunch."

My smile cracked. "That's great." I mumbled. "Have a good time."

I looked around the galley again. A dozen chicken breasts were marinating in a chimmi-churri paste on the counter. A tray of beef sat waiting to be grilled. The lobster tails were poached and sliced on plates. Large wooden bowls held a variety of salads and fresh-baked breads. Cakes cooled on a rack by the window.

I sighed. The crew would eat well that day.

Corn Salad

4 ears corn
12 cherry tomatoes, quartered
4 stalks basil, chopped fine
2 tablespoons sherry vinegar
1/4 cup olive oil
1/4 cup red onion, diced fine
1/2 teaspoon sea salt
6 grinds of black pepper

1 head Boston leaf lettuce

Bring a large pot of salted water to a boil. Cook the corn for 3 minutes. Plunge the ears into an ice water bath. When cool, cut the niblets from the core. Mix together the salad of corn, cherry tomatoes, basil, sherry vinegar, olive oil, red onion, sea salt, and pepper. Taste for acidity. Adjust as needed.

Use the Boston lettuce as a cup and place in the center of a plate. Fill with salad cup with the corn salad.

Serves 4

Chocolate Chiffon Cake

Chiffon Cake:
2/3 cup cake flour
1/3 cup cocoa powder
1 cup sugar
1-1/4 teaspoons baking powder
1/2 teaspoon baking soda
3 large eggs, separated
1/2 cup canola oil
1/3 cup water
1 teaspoon vanilla
1 large egg white
1/4 teaspoon cream of tartar

Chocolate Ganache:
1 cup whipping cream
8 oz chopped semi-sweet chocolate

Garnish:
Fresh Raspberries

Preheat oven to 325 degrees.

Sift cake flour and cocoa and mix with sugar, baking powder and baking soda in a large bowl. With a whisk, beat in egg yolks, oil, water and vanilla until smooth. In a standing mixer, beat 4 egg whites with cream of tartar until stiff. With a spatula, gently fold the egg whites into the batter.

Bake in an ungreased spring form pan for 50 minutes until a wooden skewer comes out clean. Cool for 20 minutes. Run a knife around the sides of the pan and gently unmold the cake. Cool for 30 minutes.

Bring cream to a simmer in a saucepan. Remove from heat and stir in chocolate until smooth. Cool for 5 minutes to thicken.

Spread a thin layer of ganache over the top and sides of the cake. Dip a metal spatula into hot water; dry and use to smooth icing. Place fresh raspberries on the top of the cake, a quarter-inch in from the edge in a circle.

Makes 12 slices

The Disintegration
of Dinner

The next two days were more of the same. Everyone from all three boats would arrive, unannounced and expecting full service of food and drinks. They would roar in like a hurricane, cause their damage and move on. If they weren't on our boat, we were taxiing them to the other boats and zipping back to pick them up. This was like when you read the stories of the Titanic and get to the part where the ship is actually sinking, the band is still playing, and the crew acts like nothing is wrong. That's what this charter was like. All hell was breaking loose, but we carried on.

Katie would just finish cleaning the cabins in the morning and making the beds when she'd have to start setting up for lunch. When she finished an hour later, Mister would have had a nap and destroyed the cabin, so it needed cleaning all over again.

Tom was busy ferrying the guests and taking Baby ashore to be walked. Patrick frantically conferred with the captains of *Sunchaser* and *Wave Rider* to get some inkling of what to expect, but all three crews were baffled by these people. The crew on each boat was pulled in opposite directions day after day.

And yet, still we smiled.

With all the extra guests and boats, half way through the trip I needed more fresh vegetables. I went to Patrick to discuss the logistics of having vegetables from the States sent in. He rubbed his temples and looked at the chart.

"The problem is that Mister would like to be anchored here tomorrow." He pointed to a bay on the chart. "And, the airport's on this island." He pointed to an island with a lot of blue water between it and the first destination. "Our tender will be busy with guests." He drummed his pencil up and down for a minute then walked over to his card file and started flipping through pages. "Call this guy and see if he'll deliver the order to us."

I dialed the number on the card for a local fishing guide and explained my predicament. "Nine hundred dollars," he quoted me in heavy Bahamian patois.

"What?" I couldn't keep the shock out of my voice. "It's only a few boxes of food!"

"It's a long way, baby." He wasn't about to budge. I had two thousand dollars in food ordered and already had to pay for the delivery from Florida to the Bahamas and import taxes. This was going to be an expensive order. I arranged for the delivery and called back the next day at one to make sure everything was still set.

"Whew, baby. You didn't tell me dis was gonna be such a big box." He whistled through his teeth. "Dis gonna cost more."

"What?" Again, I was incredulous. How could it possibly cost any more?

"Twelve hundred," he said. I fumed. It was robbery, but what could I do? He had my vegetables.

"Fine, just get here by three." I tried to sound tough. I'm sure I heard laughter on the other end of the phone.

A few minutes later, Patrick stormed into the galley. "The guide just called. He said the run was too long. He's adding three hundred to the bill for gas."

Words came out of my mouth that I cannot repeat.

* * * *

There was no sign of the guide's fishing boat at three, nor at four. I was pacing the galley, ringing my hands.

Patrick just laughed. "It's island time!"

I paced some more and grumbled, "I hate island time." It was perfectly fine if I were on the beach, reading and waiting for a pina colada, but when I had dinner to make in a few hours and was waiting for the ingredients to arrive, island time lost its romantic allure. I didn't want to approach that woman and explain why I would be late with her meal.

Just as I was about to crumple in the corner in tears, Patrick spotted the fishing guide through his binoculars. "He's here," he called from the wheelhouse.

I dried my hands and went outside to inspect the boxes. The tall, muscular guide greeted me with a curt nod as he tied off to our swim platform. He wore a white t-shirt with a colorful mahi-mahi curled on the front. The back had the logo, *Dinner is better in the Bahamas,* stenciled across his wide shoulders. Without a word, he effortlessly swung eight large Styrofoam cooler boxes onto the deck. He held his hand out.

"Long way, baby," he said as I handed him an envelope with his cash. He flipped through the hundred dollar bills with his thumb. "Most people tip me for my services."

Patrick stood behind me and reached in his pocket for his billfold as I tallied up the cost of the food.

$2,000 for the vegetables

$1,200 import and delivery (to the wrong island)

$1,500 to hire the fisherman to bring us the boxes

$4,700 to eat for the next few days.

I shook my head and grabbed a box to start unloading. This was one crazy trip. I would be glad when it was over.

* * * *

And, finally it was. The afternoon came when they would depart. We sailed that morning back to the larger island where their plane sat waiting for them. This time, we docked the boat without mishap. Katie delighted in packing their bags. Patrick jumped at the chance to drive them to the airport.

"Make sure you have the blender going when I get back," he said as he left. "We deserve it."

I smiled, knowing the day would disintegrate once we had our first drop of alcohol. Tom scrambled to put the covers on the furniture. Katie stripped the beds and started the first of many loads of laundry.

We reconvened in the galley. Pop, fizz. Katie opened a bottle of champagne. I hesitated for a moment, thinking we should wait for Patrick, but I really didn't want to delay Tom and Katie's fun.

Katie poured straight into our plastic glasses that normally held water and iced tea. This was no time for proper etiquette. We needed quantity, not quality.

"To freedom," Tom toasted.

Without waiting for a reply, he tipped his head back and drained the cup. All three glasses hit the table empty and Katie began pouring another round.

Tiny bubbles vibrated on my tongue and burst in my throat. The knot that had lodged itself in my neck loosened. Katie removed the clip from her hair and shook out her long locks. Tom pulled at his epaulette shirt, untucking it from his white shorts, and cranked the stereo, causing the room to shake with the bass. They jumped up and wound themselves around each other, turning the galley into a dance club. Katie grabbed another bottle. This time, the cork shot out of the neck like a flare. A stream of white fizzed out and onto the floor. Tom grabbed the bottle and stuck it in his mouth to stop the flow, guzzling a quarter of it in the process. This was going to get ugly.

I put my glass down and began serving dinner, hoping to delay the party until Patrick got back. I didn't want him to miss the fun, nor did I want to be responsible for the mayhem that was about to occur. By the look of Tom and Katie, they would need food in their bellies if this was the beginning of the evening. I hadn't made anything fancy. Even with the vegetable delivery, the extra guests had meant my stocks were running as low as my energy.

The scent of an Italian restaurant spread through the galley as I opened the oven. The sweet smell of tomatoes and basil wrapped around my senses. Cheese bubbled in the pan on top of the chicken Parmesan. I tossed linguini in sautéed garlic and olive oil and warmed the fresh-baked bread from lunch.

"Do we have any of that red still open from last night?" Katie asked, rummaging through the wine fridge. She deserved to enjoy the excess from the charter. It had been hell on all of us, but this was her first glimpse at what life on board could be like. She had survived, but barely.

"Score!" She cradled the bottle in the crook of her arm and returned to the table.

I was attacked as I set the dish down. Tom stepped in front of me and grabbed a piece of bread. I stumbled back. He dove at the dish and scooped an overflowing spoonful onto his plate.

"This is tasty," he yelled over the music. "Thanks."

The faint sound of a phone rang over the latest rendition of *Blame it on the Boogie*.

"Shh," I tried to calm the raucous around me as I picked up my cell. "Hello?" I shouted into the phone.

"There's a problem." Patrick's voice sounded far away. I turned off the stereo. "What's up?"

"Their plane's broken," his voice hesitated. "We're headed back to the boat for dinner. We'll be there in twenty minutes."

"What?" My mouth dropped open. I looked at Tom and Katie in various states of rumpled undress, glassy-eyed and already reeking of alcohol. And dinner? I had nothing left from the week and no time to prepare anything.

I looked at the casserole dish on the table; half eaten, sauce spilled over the side, all the cheese scraped off and wondered if I could serve them the leftovers.

Quick Chicken Parmesan

6 chicken breasts
4 cloves garlic, minced
1 tablespoon fresh thyme, chopped
3 tablespoons olive oil
1 teaspoon red wine vinegar
1 teaspoon sea salt

1 - 28 oz can whole tomatoes
2 tablespoons tomato paste
1 tablespoon olive oil
4 cloves garlic, minced
1 yellow onion, diced
1/4 cup fresh basil, chopped
1 teaspoon sugar
1/2 teaspoon sea salt
12 grinds black pepper

1 cup fresh grated Parmesan
6 whole sprigs of basil

    Preheat the oven to 400 degrees.
    Marinate chicken breasts in garlic, thyme, olive oil, red wine vinegar, and sea salt for 20 minutes while you make the sauce.
    Puree tomatoes, tomato paste, olive oil, garlic, onion, basil, sugar, sea salt and pepper in a blender to smooth.
    In a heavy-bottomed sauté pan, over high-heat, sear the chicken breasts for 2 minutes each side until golden. Remove and place on a cookie sheet. Roast in the oven for 15 minutes until firm to the touch.

~Continued on next page

Meanwhile, in the same pan as the chicken (do not wash, you want the flavor of the chicken in the sauce), pour the tomato sauce in and heat over medium-low for the 15 minutes the chicken is cooking.

Pour the sauce onto a lipped platter to cover the bottom. Place roasted chicken breasts on top and garnish with fresh grated Parmesan and whole sprigs of basil.

Serves 6

Love Da Tings You Do

*E*ventually, we got through it. The guests returned, but true to form, they were so caught up in themselves they didn't notice Tom's blurry eyes or that Katie spilled their wine when pouring the vintage Bordeaux.

"What the hell happened?" Patrick asked when he got back on board. One look at the two of them and he knew they were in no condition to work. "I've only been gone an hour."

I shrugged as I plated the chicken. I hadn't stooped as far as serving the leftovers, but had cut every corner I knew and winced at what I was serving. The chefs who trained me would have shaken their heads in disbelief. I had thawed two chicken breasts under water, tossed them in garlic and lemon juice, and seared them in a pan. As they finished cooking in the oven, I sautéed onions, garlic and tomatoes. I grated fresh Parmesan on top of the sauce and wiped the rims of the plates. Never in the fifteen years of being a chef had I ever served such a thrown together meal. I winced at the thought of it, but what could I do? They weren't supposed to be there that night. And, that's what I told Patrick.

"They left." I couldn't think of anything else to say.

Patrick knew what it was like. He was captain now, but it wasn't that long ago when he would have been right there beside Tom. Hell, if he hadn't taken the guests to the airport he would have been opening the bottles.

"You didn't even wait for me!" Patrick's voice squeaked.

I had no response.

Patrick shook his head. "Three hours. We just need to get through the next three hours."

And we did. We spilled and slurred our way through dinner, said our goodbyes again, and Patrick took them back to the airport where their plane was fixed. And they left, out of our lives forever.

* * * *

That night, Patrick and I lay in bed talking. It was pitch black in the room. We whispered, discussing what went wrong and what went right.

"Trial by fire," Patrick said.

"We got through it."

"Painfully," he scoffed.

"It could have been a lot worse."

He scoffed, "How?"

I laughed along with him. "We didn't sink."

"Suck it up, Katie!" We heard Tom yell from their cabin across the hall. The thin walls of the boat meant there was little privacy between the four of us.

"I didn't go to university for four years to clean toilets, Tom," Katie screamed.

I knew where this fight was going.

"Then leave! I like it here."

"Sure, you get to be in the sun all day jet-skiing and playing in the water. I'm stuck downstairs in the cabins cleaning things that are already clean."

They weren't the first couple to have this fight.

"Is she going to make it?" Patrick whispered.

We had lived on boats long enough to know that you had to whisper if you didn't want everyone knowing every little thing you said.

"I hope so," I whispered back. "The first trip is always the biggest adjustment." And, this hadn't been the easiest introduction. I thought about my own first trip and how many things had gone wrong. "She'll get there."

* * *

The next week was our own. We still had a lot of work to do, but it was on a normal, nine to five-ish schedule. After the fight we overheard, Patrick made sure Katie got some time on the beach and in the water. She brightened immediately. It always amazed me how a few minutes of fun could wipe away hours of toil when guests were aboard. After a good night's sleep, some sunshine, and a little encouragement, Katie was smiling again and her fight with Tom seemed to be forgotten.

For me, the relaxed schedule meant time to explore the food of the Bahamas. On our first afternoon after the charter, I entered the yacht club bar to ask where I could buy fresh baked coconut bread. It was a favorite of mine and I wanted to introduce it to our crew.

"You gots to see Vivian," Wade, a charter fisherman told me. He was a large man with pitch-black curls shaved close to his head. "She makes de best on island. Jus' follow de road past de airport. She's mindin' de store."

I walked the only road leading away from the yacht club. No need to worry about asking for detailed directions. The sun beat down, reminding me once again that I was in the tropics. Fluffy clouds underlined in lilac splattered the sky, looking like the cream I'd just whipped for key lime tarts.

I passed a small one-room schoolhouse with six island children reciting a verse inside.

"Ring-a-ring-rosies.

A pocket full of Posies.

Hush! Hush! Hush! Hush!

We're all tumbled down!"

Their voices carried through the still air. Colorful cottage homes with hibiscus bushes blooming bright yellow and orange lined the road. Breathing in the floral perfume, I wondered why my plants in Lauderdale were never laden with so many flowers. Laundry hung from lines, flapping in the breeze.

I passed the one-room medical clinic. *Doctor on island Friday,* read a sign nailed to the tree. I hoped no one had an emergency until then. A small Baptist church marked the turn toward the airstrip. Across the creek I could see the general store.

Upon arriving, Vivian greeted me from behind the counter. "Good day to you, baby." She wore a New York Yankees t-shirt. A Yamaha ball cap shielded her face, but couldn't hide the bright smile.

"Wade sent me down. He says you make the best coconut bread on the island."

"He's right about that."

"I was hoping you could teach me how," I said.

She squealed with laughter. "Well child, let me sees. I gots to get someone to grate a coconut for me."

"I have a bag of pre-shredded on the boat if that makes it easier," I volunteered.

Her face twisted to one side and she pursed her lips, her eyes squeezed shut as if she just bit into a lemon. "No, you'se have to use fresh grated coconut. Lesson number one." She laughed again shaking her head. What do these crazy white girls know about anything, she seemed to think. "Tomorrow's the island barbecue and I gots to cook for that. Then the mailboat comes the next day, and I's have to unpack it. The next day after that we's make some bread."

Patiently, I waited on the boat. Each morning, Tom and Patrick washed the boat while Katie did laundry and I made lunch. By one o'clock, we were in the water swimming, wake-boarding, and kayaking. We returned to work in the late afternoon to wrap everything up, clean the toys, and make dinner. We ate each night under the stars on the top deck and watched a movie before retiring, exhausted from the sun.

One afternoon, Patrick and I took the tender to shore. We walked along a stretch of beach that curved around the crescent bay where the boat was anchored. The clarity of the water made it seem like we were looking into an aquarium.

"Look there." Patrick pointed to a dozen stingrays trailing each other through the shallows. Just beyond, a school of mullet darted in and out of each other's way. We walked along the sun-baked sand past a variety of shells washed onto the beach. Patrick bent down and picked up a lacquered brown oval.

"This is a kauri shell." He turned it over in his hand to show the clam-like opening. "I used to see these in Hawaii when I lived there, but never in such great shape."

"It's beautiful." Coming from Canada, I had never seen one. "And so shiny. I always thought people buffed and painted them to look this perfect. I didn't realize they came out of the ocean like that." I ran my hand over the smooth surface. Even after eight years of yachting, there was still so much about the ocean I didn't know.

* * * *

On Friday afternoon, I retraced my steps through the village with a faster pace. The sweet smell of coconut wafted out the screen door when I arrived at Vivian's. A wooden bowl with a pile of white, flaked coconut sat on the countertop along with a generic five-pound bag of flour. "I's already baked all mornin' but we's can make another batch." She threw her head back and let out a booming laugh. "Everybody love when I make bread."

Without measuring, Vivian poured flour onto the counter, creating a white powder mountain. She thrust a thick fist into the center to make a well. From a plastic container she scooped large handfuls of sugar into the center. "We's like our bread sweet. Just like the women here." Again, she howled.

"This is a breakfast bread then?"

"No child. This here is for anytime. My coconut bread don't last around here 'til morning."

She cut open two envelopes of yeast and poured them into a coffee mug of warm water. She hummed while she pinched some of the sugar from the pile into the mug. "This here I just set aside for a minute to start bubblin'. It works best that way."

Vivian turned back to her pile and scooped a large wooden spoon full of soft butter from a tin on the counter. With a flick of her wrist, she sent up a flour cloud as the butter buried itself in the center of the well. She grabbed the wooden bowl of coconut and scraped the wet pile into the flour.

By now, the coffee mug had a beige cloud of yeast bubbling on the surface. She poured the cup into the well and began scooping the sides of flour up and into the center. She shook salt into the mixture. Her bosom jiggled as the dough on the counter began to take shape.

"You gots to love the tings you do for people." Vivian used her large upper frame to knead the dough. The muscles in her arms told her story of just how many loaves of coconut bread she had rolled in her life. "I just love doing these tings. It isn't work if you love it." She began to sing. "Junkanoos a comin'. Just around the corner." She stretched out, pushing forward with her palms. She gathered up the dough and hugged it back toward her body. She moved in rhythm to her humming.

"Love. Dat is what you taste in my bread. It's the love." She caressed the ball of dough like she would a newborn baby's head. "Now, I just leaves this to set for an hour or so until it's twice this size. Then I shape it into two dough pans and set it to rise again. After another hour, I bake it." She turned to the stove and grabbed one of the loaves off the cooling rack. "And this is what you gets. Coconut bread." Her smile beamed like the rays of the sun.

Vivian placed a still warm golden loaf in my hands and handed me a bag with two more. "You'se take these to your friends on the boat and tell them this here is the taste of the Bahamas."

I smiled. I too, loved da tings she did.

Key Lime Tarts

Crust:
1-1/2 cups graham crackers crumbs
2 tablespoons sugar
1/2 cup butter, melted

Filling:
4 egg yolks
1 can (14 ounces) sweetened condensed milk
8-12 Key limes, juiced (to make 2/3 cup juice), zest kept from 2 of the limes

Topping:
1 cup heavy cream
2 tablespoons confectioner's sugar
1 teaspoon vanilla

Crust:
   Preheat the oven to 325 degrees.
   Place the graham cracker crumbs in a food processor. Add the melted butter and sugar and pulse until combined. Press 2 tablespoons of the mixture into the bottom of 12 muffins tins lined with muffin papers, forming an even layer on the bottom. Bake the crusts for 15 minutes. Remove from the oven and cool.

Filling:
   In a standing mixer with the wire whisk attachment, whip the egg yolks and lime zest at high speed for 5 minutes until fluffy. Gradually add the condensed milk and continue to whip for 4 minutes until thick. Lower the mixer speed and slowly add the lime juice until incorporated.
   Pour the mixture into the crust and bake for 15 minutes, or until the filling has just set. Cool for 10 minutes and then refrigerate for 20 minutes.

Topping:
   Whip the cream and confectioners' sugar until stiff. Whip in vanilla. Evenly spread the whipped cream on top of the tarts, and place in the freezer for 15 minutes prior to serving.

Makes 12 tarts

Vivian's Coconut Bread

1 cup warm water
2 packages yeast
1 teaspoon sugar
1-1/2 cups grated coconut with the water (about two coconuts OR $\frac{1}{2}$ cup grated dry coconut from a bag and 1 cup coconut milk)
5 cups flour (amount of flour may vary depending on how much water is inside the coconuts)
1/2 stick soft butter
1/2 cup sugar
1 teaspoon sea salt
1 egg, whisked

    Combine warm water, yeast and 1 teaspoon sugar in a large bowl; let stand 5 minutes until yeast begins to bubble and look fluffy. Mix the rest of the ingredients in until a soft dough forms. Turn dough out onto a lightly floured surface. Knead until smooth and soft (about 10 minutes); add extra flour to prevent dough from sticking to your hands or the surface.

    Place dough back in bowl, lightly spray with non-stick spray and cover with plastic wrap. Let stand 1-1/2 hours to allow dough to rise until doubled.

    Turn dough out onto a lightly floured counter. Divide dough into two. Working with one half at a time, roll dough out into a log. Place into a bread pan that has been lightly sprayed with non-stick spray. Brush the top of the bread with a whisked egg to glaze the top. Cover and let rise for 45 minutes until it has doubled in size.

    Pre-heat oven to 350 degrees. With a sharp knife, make five long diagonal slashes on the top of the bread.

    Bake for 40 minutes until golden brown. Cool on a wire rack.

Makes 2 loaves

The Cook-Off

" There'll be two children on this charter," Patrick told us a week later. "Luke is five and Lizzie is turning three." He looked at me and raised an eyebrow. "Little kids." Patrick had seen my awkwardness with children before.

Don't get me wrong, I love children: other people's children. My nieces, for example, are two of my favorite people, but I have trouble talking and playing with them. Where Patrick just walks in the room, makes a funny noise, and they fall over themselves laughing, I think long and hard before I tell a joke and they just stare at me bewildered. I sound funny in my head, but apparently not so to a four and six-year-old.

And they aren't the only ones. Kids run to "Uncle Patrick" to play, yet have to be scolded by their parents before they'll acknowledge me in the room. Usually, I can sit quietly and hide while Patrick entertains them, but a weeklong charter, sequestered on a boat, with only one hundred and ten feet for them to run around… Eventually, they'd head into the galley to explore—and yell, and bang pots, and smash things.

The galley is a place of boiling water, sharp knives, crystal glasses, and hot surfaces. Not exactly friendly to tender little hands.

"Maybe they'll stay in the guest quarters," I said.

Patrick shook his head. "Do you know *anything* about children?"

"I love kids," Katie's face lit up.

Somehow I knew she would. Her cheery disposition screamed of camp counselor. "Good. They're all yours!"

Day One came and I felt fairly confident I could skirt the little hellions. They would be too excited about swimming to venture into the galley. If I kept my head down and avoided the guest areas I'd be safe.

Katie and I had spent the last two weeks practicing carrying plates and trays. Her service had improved dramatically, and I was much less worried about her on this trip. Having kids to play with would let her shine.

This time, Tom drove the tender to pick up the guests. He approached the boat slowly and expertly nudged the boat up to the yacht from a wide angle. Parents and kids were offloaded.

Katie and I stood above on the aft deck. Patrick was already in full fun-guy mode when they stepped onto the swim platform. He reached down and swung a small child with dark ringlets and almond-shaped eyes the color of chocolate onto his shoulders. He swayed her back and forth, with each step pretending the boat was rocking.

"Whoa," he called as he sidestepped one way, dipping low. "Hold on tight," he said as he crossed the other way. "The waves are craz-z-zy." He stuttered his words and shook his head.

Lizzie giggled with delight and hugged his head tight. "Whee! Do it again!"

Luke held Patrick's hand, waiting his turn. But the game changed suddenly as Patrick clicked his heels together, straightened his back and saluted. "Permission to come aboard, Captain?" he asked the little boy with all seriousness.

The boy's eyes shone as he looked at Patrick and nodded. "Aye, aye."

Patrick marched military style up the back stairs to where we waited.

He leaned over to whisper to Luke. "This is Victoria." From behind his hand he said loud enough for everyone to hear, "She made us possum sandwiches for lunch."

"Eww, yuck," the little girl squealed. She scrunched up her dollop of a nose and crinkled her forehead. Mom and Dad hung back smiling, probably relieved to have found a babysitter so early in the trip. "I hate possum!" She crossed her arms over her chest and stamped her tiny foot.

"Well, you'll go awfully hungry here then." I tried to play along. I should have known not to attempt a joke.

The little girl's bottom lip began to quiver. Tears filled her eyes. She let out a wail that sounded like it may have come from a possum or maybe a howler monkey. My eyes grew wide and I looked at Patrick, pleading with him to help. He just shook his head and rolled his eyes.

Mom stepped in. "I'm sure she has chicken fingers, too." The woman cradled the little girl in a hug and smiled up at me. "She was just kidding." She sounded like Mary Poppins, all soothing and nurturing. The little girl sniffled and stopped crying. Even I felt better.

The husband, an athletic-looking, dark-haired man wearing a Chicago Cubs cap, placed his hand on Luke's shoulder. "Come on, Champ. Let's go see what toys are on board." He clapped Patrick on the back as he passed.

As Patrick took the husband and kids to the bow, I toured the wife through the boat and showed her to her cabin. "We'll be happy to unpack for you while you have lunch," I said.

She shook her chestnut bob. "Don't be silly, I can do that." She pulled shorts and t-shirts from her bag and placed them in the drawers. I showed her where the life jackets and escape hatches were in each room. "Are these child-sized?" She picked up one of the lifejackets to inspect it.

"Yes, we switched out the two in the kids cabin."

"Thank you."

I liked these people. They seemed normal.

"Mom!" Luke roared into the room. "Even the taps are gold!" He grabbed his mom's hand and pulled her into the bathroom. "Look!" He climbed from the toilet to the counter and straddled the sink, planting both his hands on the mirror to steady himself. His mom laughed and lifted him down, leaving behind two handprints that screamed *Luke was here.*

"I checked every room," he said proudly. "They're all the same."

Ugh! There goes hours of polishing, I thought.

I left the wife to unpack and headed to the aft deck to confer with Patrick. I found him on the swim platform with Lizzie. He'd filled the Rubbermaid bin we used to rinse dive gear with water and was sitting inside with the little girl. With his upper body he shook the bin back and forth. Bubbles foamed on the surface of the water. Lizzie giggled.

"What are you guys doing?" I asked, somewhat confused about this game.

The husband stood beside me. He had his SLR camera out taking pictures. "Patrick showed us the Jacuzzi up top, but said it was for adults." His camera captured the activity with rapid-fire shots. "So, he set up a kid's tub."

Where did he come up with this stuff?

* * * *

I retreated to the galley to squeeze limes and toast cumin for a Latin marinade. I had planned a tropical lunch to welcome the family to the islands.

"What are you doing?" A small voice inquired.

I looked around, but couldn't see anyone. A mop of blond hair popped up behind the marble counter-top.

"Can I help?" Luke used the cupboard handles as ladder-rungs to climb. He scooted across the polished surface, digging his heels in and scooching his bottom, like a crab scurrying across sand. "I always help Mom at home. I'm a good cook."

"Well, honey. I'll bet you are a big help, but I have to make lunch for your mom and dad so…" I stumbled. Would a five-year old take a hint?

"I'll help. I can stir." He didn't seem to be leaving.

"Wouldn't you like to go see the jet skis with Tom?" I asked, trying not to sound like I was pleading.

"Nah, we have two at home."

Patrick leaned in the doorframe, his arms crossed, a smile spread across his face. "I see you have a sous-chef."

"What would you like for lunch?" I asked Luke, resigned to have to deal with the kids.

"Macaroni and cheese," Luke said. "It's my favorite. I can stir the sauce."

I sighed, knowing there was no escape. I filled a stockpot with water and placed it on the stove to boil. "This is very hot. You must be very careful," I warned Luke in a voice reminiscent of my second-grade teacher.

He looked at me like I had just announced the sky is blue. "I know. I told you, I'm a good cook."

I nodded, noting there was no need to talk to Luke like he was a five-year old.

I pulled mozzarella out of the fridge. He grabbed it out of my hand and started grating before I could even warn him about the sharp edges.

"Do you have bacon? I like bacon in my macaroni." This kid was a gourmand. Maybe he wasn't so bad after all.

I sautéed bacon with garlic and made a roux to stabilize the cheese sauce. We simmered the milk with a touch of grated nutmeg and some fresh thyme. Luke didn't seem to be turning his nose up at any of the un-boxed mac and cheese-like products.

I pulled a stool over to the stove and Luke stirred the pasta in. He was right. He was good at this.

"I'm in charge of making breakfasts on Sunday for Mom and Dad," Luke informed me.

I placed the baking dish in the oven and Luke took the spatula to the sink. "Mom, says I have to clean up my own mess." He balanced himself on the edge of the sink and washed the spoon.

As the mac and cheese baked, Luke sat on the counter, telling me about the fire trucks and cars he played with at home. "I wasn't allowed to bring them all." He frowned slightly. "But, I stuck two of my favorites in Lizzie's bag."

I still had a full "grown-up" meal to prepare. I chopped on one end of the counter while Luke sat at the other.

Finally, the time came to pull the macaroni from the oven. Luke smiled a toothy grin. He jumped down and ran to call his parents to the table. I plated two macaroni and cheeses for the children. I sliced *mojo*-marinated chicken breasts and fanned them around a plate for the adults. I towered a pile of baby spinach and mango salad in the center and scattered toasted cashews around the plate.

Katie wiped the rims and delivered lunch to the guests without spilling a drop. She returned two minutes later. "Two more plates of macaroni and cheese, please."

"The kids ate it all?" I asked surprised.

"No, for mom and dad," she said. "They all want the kid's food."

I tasted a spoonful of Luke's macaroni. It was good, I couldn't blame them. This was going to be a different kind of trip. Not only was I going to learn how to play with kids, but I had just had my first cook-off with a five-year old—and lost.

Luke's Five-Year Old Macaroni and Cheese

1 pound elbow macaroni
6 slices bacon, diced small
4 cloves garlic, minced
2 tablespoons flour
4 cups milk
1 teaspoon sea salt
12 grinds of black pepper
1/8 teaspoon nutmeg
1 tablespoon fresh thyme
1 cup cheddar, grated
1/2 cup mozzarella, grated
1/3 cup Parmesan, grated
1/2 cup breadcrumbs
2 tablespoons melted butter
2 tablespoons chopped parsley

Preheat oven to 350 degrees.

Cook pasta in a large pot of boiling salted water for 5 minutes until just tender but still firm to the bite. Drain.

Sauté bacon in a heavy-bottomed pot over medium heat for 5 minutes. Once it begins to crisp, add garlic for one minute. Stir in flour. Slowly add milk, whisking constantly. Season with sea salt, pepper, nutmeg and thyme. Simmer for 5 minutes to incorporate flavors. Stir occasionally. Stir in cheeses and remove from heat. Stir in pasta.

Mix breadcrumbs, butter and parsley.

Place macaroni in a greased gratin dish. Top with breadcrumbs. Bake for 20 minutes. Pre-heat broiler. Place under broiler for 1 minute until topping is crisp and golden brown.

Serves 8

Mojo-Marinated Grilled Chicken

Marinade:
6 cloves garlic, minced
2 teaspoons sea salt
24 grinds black pepper
1 tablespoon cumin
2 oranges, juiced
1 lemon, juiced
1 lime, juiced
1 cup onion, minced
1/4 scotch bonnet, minced (more or less depending on heat tolerance)
2 teaspoons oregano
1 cup olive oil

12 chicken thighs, boneless and skinless
1 lime
1 tablespoon cilantro, chopped

The day before:
In a bowl, whisk the marinade ingredients together. Pour the marinade over the chicken thighs and mix to ensure marinade is coating the chicken. Refrigerate overnight, turning occasionally.

The Next Day:
Preheat a grill to medium-high heat.
Remove the thighs from marinade and pat dry with paper towel. Place them on a heated grill for 5 minutes each side and cook to an internal temperature of 160 degrees, until juices run clear.
Place on a platter and squeeze one lime over the chicken.
Sprinkle chopped cilantro over the thighs and serve.

Serves 6

The Galley Explosion

*A*s far as the family was concerned, the trip was going well. We spent the week finding new bays to explore and new beaches to comb. Every day, the family ate breakfast together while I packed a picnic, then everyone headed to the beach. I barbecued and the kids swam. Tom drove Luke around on the jet-ski, and Katie played in the sand with Lizzie. It felt more like we were all vacationing together. By sunset, we were back on the boat, the kids and crew exhausted. I made dinner for the parents while mom put Luke and Lizzie to bed.

On the fourth morning of the trip, I stepped into the shower before heading upstairs to cook breakfast. It was a tight upright box, and I bumped my funny bone on the frame on the way in. "Oww," I yelped.

"Are you okay in there?" Tom called from beyond the thin walls of the bathroom we all shared.

"Fine," I muttered, embarrassed and mad at how small the boat was. I turned on the water to drown out my thoughts and was hit by icy-cold water.

"Oww," I screamed this time and leaped out of the cubicle. On the way out, I tripped on the frame and crashed to the floor, smashing into the door on the way down. I made quite the ruckus. Within seconds, both Patrick and Tom were pounding on the door.

"Are you okay in there?" Tom called again.

"Do you need help?" Patrick asked.

Madder and more embarrassed than before, I yelled, "I hate this boat!"

* * * *

"Who's ready for an adventure?" Patrick asked the kids at breakfast.

"I am!" Luke's hand shot up.

"Me, too!" Lizzie jumped from her chair.

"Have you guys ever seen pigs swim?" I asked, knowing what Patrick had in mind.

"Pigs can't swim!" Lizzie squealed.

The husband laughed and reached over to ruffle Lizzie's hair. "I think you mean they can't fly."

"I wanna see the flying pigs!" Lizzie wailed.

I laughed. The kid was cute. "Well, we'd better get going."

The wife slathered sunscreen on the children. Tom and Patrick brought the tender around, and I packed waters and a bag of celery sticks into a cooler. On the swim platform, I set the cooler down and grabbed the bow of the tender to steady it as the parents and kids clamored inside.

"Ready for fun?" Patrick asked the group.

"Ready," everyone agreed.

I unhooked the bowline from the cleat and pushed off as I stepped into the boat.

Patrick cranked the wheel to the left, and we circled away from the boat. The sun blazed high in the sky. Salt spray showered onto my skin as we skimmed across the flat water.

"Look, Mommy." Lizzie pointed ahead. "It's Ariel's swimming pool."

She was right. The ocean was as blue as a mermaid's bath.

Patrick switched seats with Tom so he could drive as Patrick scooped Lizzie up and placed her on his knee. "You know, we may just see a mermaid or two today."

Lizzie's eyes lit up. Luke's narrowed. "I thought we're going to see pigs?"

"We are." Patrick turned to Luke. "But, you never know what you'll find out here on the high seas." Patrick looked left and then right over his shoulder and whispered. "We might even see pirates!"

It was hot in the tender, and I could already feel my skin turning pink. I was glad to see the white sand of the beach close-by. Three light pink piglets bolted from under the shade of the seagrape trees and galloped down the beach.

—— VICTORIA ALLMAN ——

"Look!" I pointed.

Everyone shifted in their seat to watch the pigs splash into the water and begin doggy-paddling toward us. Patrick and I had been here before and seen the show. The pigs were feral, but were used to tourists feeding them. Over the years, they had become bold and now would swim out to greet the boats, eager for their meal.

Patrick moved to the bow as Tom slowed the boat. He leapt over the side of the tender and held the boat in place as a brown spotted large adult pig lumbered into the clear water after the piglets.

Lizzie yelped and her mother cradled her tight. The little girl twisted in her mother's lap to get the best view. The pigs were only a few feet from the tender and closing in fast.

"Victoria, hand me the food." Patrick held his hand out while keeping an eye on the approaching swine. An even larger black pig charged through the shallows toward us. He looked like a defensive tackle. He must have been two hundred pounds, at least.

I reached down to grab the cooler and my hand grazed the floor. I looked down at the empty space beside my feet. The bag was not there. I had left it on the swim platform. I took a deep breath. "Um … Patrick."

He must have heard the dread in my voice. I didn't want to be the one to tell him. Patrick whipped his head around and glared at me. "What?"

I gulped. The pigs advanced. "We don't have any food for them."

Normally, Patrick tried not to let the guests see him panic. But there was no hiding the look in his eyes. It only took a second for Patrick to turn, gage the distance between his body in the water and the hungry pigs and start to push himself out of the water. His deltoids flexed and his left leg kicked out.

Lizzie cried out again, "Mommy!" She pointed to the black pig who had quickly caught up to the group.

He was inches from Patrick and moving fast. Patrick curled his upper body over the gunwale to dive into the boat. The seat of his board shorts stuck out. As his legs flicked up and out of the water, the mouth of the pig opened and clamped down on the blue fabric. The sound of the fabric tearing was drowned out by the howl coming from Patrick's mouth.

I sat stunned, mouth-open, just staring. Lizzie giggled.

Luke looked astonished. "Cool!"

Patrick lay on the floor of the tender, his blinding white bottom exposed to the brutal Bahamian sun. He looked shocked, but recovered quickly in front of the kids. "Did you see that?" He asked Luke. "Victoria just fed me to the pigs for lunch."

* * * *

That afternoon, Tom, Katie and I took the family to the beach while Patrick stayed behind to work on the plumbing. We'd been having trouble with it ever since the engine room had flooded on the first trip. The pressure was low and had messed with the toilet system, and now the hot water was being affected. This wasn't something we wanted the guests to become aware of, or deal with.

When we returned from the beach I headed into the galley to start dinner, relieved to find hot water flowing through the tap.

"Victoria, stop making dinner!" The husband announced, as he strode into the galley. He picked up an apron and fitted the strap over his head. "I'm going to cook tonight."

"You're cooking?" The words slipped out of my mouth before I could shape them into something less incredulous-sounding.

"Yes, I made dinner for my wife the night I asked her to marry me and now, every year for our anniversary, I make my legendary angel hair Napoli." He spoke in an exaggerated Italian accent. He pinched his index finger and thumb together, lifting them to his lips and kissing the air. "It's what made her fall in love with me."

"Would you like some help?"

"No, no. I've got it all under control." He looked around the galley. "Where do you keep the pots?"

I pointed to the cupboard under the stove. He reached down and yanked, but it didn't open.

"Wait!" I cried, but I was too late. He yanked harder on the door handle and I heard the hinge pop. I kept all my cupboards latched when we were at anchor so they wouldn't open when we rolled.

I tried to be diplomatic. "Maybe I'll just stick around, so I can learn your recipe." I demonstrated how to open the locks without pulling them out of the hinges. I felt guilty. Not only were we being paid to hang out on the beach all day having fun, but now I wasn't even making dinner for them.

"Great." His face broke into a grin. "You'll love this." He slammed the heavy-bottomed stockpot onto my ceramic stovetop. I stopped my face from cringing as I watched the corner shatter into a spider-web of tiny cracks.

"First, I need garlic." He held his hand out while I reached into the wicker basket on the counter to grab a head. I guessed I would be the sous-chef in his romantic dinner. "A can of tomatoes, a bunch of basil, capers, black olives and Parmesan." He ran down his list of ingredients, counting them off on his fingers, as I scurried around him in the small space.

He spotted my knife rack in the corner and grabbed my favorite chef's knife, the one I had spent hours sharpening to a fine edge. With one fluid motion, he stabbed it into the top of the aluminum can of tomatoes.

My mouth opened, but no words came out. The only sound in the room was the screeching of metal. I stared as he wrenched it back and forth peeling back the lid. "No need for fancy gadgets like can openers and garlic presses," he said proudly.

I turned my back to fill a pot with water. I stared out the window and started to count to ten slowly. I turned back to the stove just in time to see him scraping the bottom of my new Teflon pan with a pair of steel tongs as he stirred the garlic in olive oil.

"You want to make sure the garlic doesn't burn." He sounded like he was rehearsing for the Food Network.

My teeth clenched together. It was, ultimately, just a pan, after all. I could buy a new one.

With the flick of his wrist, he spewed tomatoes from the jagged opening in the can, toward the pan. Most of it made it, the rest ended up splattered across the back of the stove. Without hesitation, he picked up the delicate white glass-polishing towel and wiped up the bright red juice, only getting half of the excess.

As the sauce sputtered on the stove, the husband dumped a package of angel hair into the salted water. He stirred once and went back to chopping the capers and black olives. After five minutes, he returned his attention to the boiling water. "Do you know how to tell if the pasta is done?"

I was about to answer with the obvious, *taste it,* when he plucked a strand from the pot and threw it against my polished stainless steel backsplash. The noodle stuck to the wall and slowly slithered down the shiny surface, leaving a trail like a slug.

He deemed the pasta ready and poured the pot into a colander in the far sink. But before all the water had drained from the angel hair, he lifted the colander and dribbled starchy water across my countertop as he dumped the pasta into the saucepan. "I like to mix the pasta and sauce together." Sauce splattered everywhere. The steel tongs went back into the pan. "Plain noodles with sauce on top is not the Italian way." Again, the Italian accent had crept into his voice, but this time he sounded more like a character from the Sopranos than a man from Florence. I wondered if he knew he was from the mid-west.

He grabbed a bread knife and cut slices of the crusty baguette I had baked that morning to go with his meal. He swept the crumbs from the counter to the floor. The galley was exploding before my eyes.

"Voila," he said. "Dinner for everyone."

"It looks fantastic." I wasn't humoring him. It did look tasty.

He took the two plates from my hand and twirled the noodles in a pile.

"And the best part of this meal." He held the two bowl of pasta up for me to see. "Because I did the cooking, I don't have to clean up."

Angel Hair Napoli

1/4 cup olive oil
1 onion, diced fine
4 cloves garlic, sliced thin
1/2 teaspoon sea salt
12 grinds black pepper
1 can (28 ounces) diced tomatoes
1 teaspoon sugar
1/2 cup kalamata olives, pitted and sliced to the size of the capers
1/4 cup capers, roughly chopped
1/2 teaspoon sea salt
1(1 pound) package angel hair pasta
1 bunch basil, chopped (1/4 cup)
1/2 cup freshly shaved Parmesan cheese

Bring a large pot of water (2 gallons) to a boil with 2 tablespoons sea salt. Meanwhile, in a separate heavy-bottomed skillet on medium-high, sauté the onion, garlic, sea salt and black pepper in olive oil for 5 minutes until onions turn golden. In a blender, purée the tomatoes for 30 seconds. Pour tomatoes into the onions and reduce heat to low. Stir in sugar. Simmer for 20 minutes, stirring occasionally. Add black olives, capers, and sea salt and simmer for another 10 minutes. Taste for seasoning.

Cook the pasta in the salted water until al dente. Drain well.

Mix basil into the pasta sauce and pour the pasta into the saucepot. Stir well to coat the pasta with the sauce.

Serve with shaved Parmesan on the side.

Serves 6

In Charge

We made it through our second charter and were heading into our third. After the family left, we had a week's turnaround time to get the boat washed, buy more food, and start over again.

This time we welcomed three couples on board. The birthday boy was a CEO of a large, well-known Wall Street company. Patrick was excited to have him on board.

"This guy's used to getting what he wants," he told us in our pre-charter meeting. "He has guys doing his bidding everywhere and is known to be a hard-ass in business."

Katie blanched and swallowed hard. "What if something goes wrong?"

That was a fair question. We were still only a few months into this boat and, although the service was running smoother with each trip, problems with the boat kept popping up at the worst times. Just the day before, the water maker stopped working and we had been without water on board all afternoon while Patrick and Tom tinkered with the machine. Not only did we not have showers, but we couldn't do dishes, wash linens, or fill buckets to scrub the decks. All work stopped as abruptly as running aground until it was fixed. Eventually, Patrick and Tom got it going again, but neither was confident how long the fix would last.

* * * *

The group arrived at seven on Friday night. The CEO led the way, tugging at the knot in his tie as he came up the gangway. He had slipped it over his head by the time he reached the aft deck.

"Good evening, sir," Patrick started on his welcome speech.

He looked Patrick in the eye and shook his hand. "Captain." He clasped Patrick's shoulder like they were golf buddies. "Are you ready for us?"

"Yes, sir." Patrick nodded.

"Weather?"

"It should be a great week," Patrick said. "Sunny and calm."

"The wind?"

"It's usually light in the morning and picks up in the afternoon."

"Good, good." With the minutes of the meeting finished, the CEO turned his attention to me. "I'll have a Bombay Sapphire and tonic." He removed his Armani jacket and handed it to Katie. "Two limes." He turned back to Patrick. "We'll leave the dock in twenty minutes." Without waiting for a response, he made his way to the sundeck calling over his shoulder, "And, we'll have dinner in an hour."

His friends smiled and mumbled hellos as they followed him up the stairs.

We stood staring at one another before scattering an instant later. Katie ran to pour his drink. Tom scurried to loosen the lines as Patrick hurried to start the engines. I bolted for the galley. There was no doubt who was in charge of this trip.

* * * *

"I want to go kite-surfing after lunch," the CEO told Patrick the next morning.

Katie and I were setting up the breakfast buffet. The man's passport told us he was fifty-two, but I found it difficult to believe there were men half his age in as great shape as he.

"The wind should be out of the east and perfect for it," Patrick said.

He'd risen early that morning to check the weather and to be prepared for any questions the CEO might have. On other boats, we'd had movie stars on board and music giants, none of whom impressed Patrick. Rarely star-struck, especially after getting to know them, Patrick treated each guest the same. This man was different. This man he wanted to impress.

"We'll use the twelve-meter kite once the wind picks up." The man consulted his blackberry and pulled up his schedule. "Ten o'clock we'll go paddle-boarding. Then lunch at one and kiting in the afternoon." He looked up to catch my eye. "A light lunch of crab Louis and clubhouse sandwiches, no butter on the toast, and dinner tonight of grilled fish and a soup." He clicked his PDA off and placed it on the table beside his juice glass. "No later than eight o'clock."

He might have been on holiday and supposed to be relaxing, but he still controlled the day and ran it like a business meeting.

His wife rolled her eyes and laughed. "Do you want to ask anyone else what they'd like?"

He raised one eyebrow and looked at his other guests.

"Sounds great," the other man agreed like an eager puppy. "Whatever you plan is always good."

The CEO smiled and clapped his friend on the back. "You'll love the kiting. It's a rush."

The friend nodded so fast I thought he would sustain whiplash. "It'll be awesome."

The CEO switched his attention back to me. "We'll have egg white omelets with feta and tomatoes."

His wife groaned and laughed again. "I hope that's what everyone would like."

They nodded in agreement.

"Of course," I said. The man knew what he wanted, which would make this trip easy if he chose things we could do—and painful if we didn't have what he wanted on board.

* * * *

The next day, the man scheduled paddle-boarding again in the morning and kite-boarding in the afternoon. He ordered meals for precisely eight a.m., two o'clock, and eight p.m. He awakened early, ran on the treadmill for an hour while talking on his phone to his personal assistant, and ate breakfast as he typed e-mails; all before anyone else was up and around.

"How about spear-fishing?" Patrick offered at breakfast on the third morning.

"What'll we find?" He clearly wanted all the facts before agreeing.

"The Bahamas are good for grouper and hogfish." Patrick had been free-diving all winter on our afternoons off. I would snorkel above, watching while he practiced how long he could stay under water. Slowly, with each dive, he progressed from a minute to almost three, enough time to search for large fish, steady his aim, and shoot. His spear would fly through the water and, if he were lucky, would skewer the target. He would then flutter-kick his way to the surface with his catch and toss it into the tender before descending again. He was getting good at it, but it was far from easy and he returned more times than not, empty-handed.

He loved it though and thought it would interest the CEO. The man pursed his lips and nodded, listening to Patrick explain what they would do.

"Okay, we'll go at three, after lunch." He looked at me. "I'll bring you grouper to cook tonight." It wasn't a question of *if* he caught something, the outcome was a given.

I didn't have the courage to tell him how often I had been told I would be brought dinner back and how few times people were successful. I decided I better pull some chicken from the freezer, just in case.

That afternoon, the three men went spear-fishing with Patrick and Tom while the women stayed onboard sun tanning. When I delivered a tray of pineapple and strawberries to the already bronzed women, I heard the wife of the CEO tell the group, "It's not like he's going through a mid-life crisis." She smiled at me as she reached for a slice of fruit. "He's always been like this."

"Aren't you worried about him hurting himself?" one woman asked.

"There's not much I can do to dissuade him. He thinks he's indestructible." She took a bite of pineapple. "I don't think he'll ever grow up."

I left the tray of fruit on the table beside the lounging women and went back to the galley, thinking about what they said.

* * * *

As the returning tender approached the aft deck, I went out to catch their lines. Sure enough, the CEO threw two six-pound groupers onto the aft deck like he'd been doing this his whole life.

"We'll have these lightly seared with sautéed vegetables and rice." He thought a moment. "Something Asian." He walked up the stairs.

I stared. "How'd he get those so fast?"

Patrick shrugged. "Even the fish know he always gets what he wants."

While the men showered and changed for dinner, I spoke to Patrick in the galley. "You know, you're a lot like that man."

A smile played in his voice. "Really?"

"Sure." I picked up my filleting knife and began butchering the grouper. "You do all those things he's doing this trip. Paddle-boarding, diving, spear-fishing. He's paying a lot of money to be here doing them, but you get to do them anytime you want." I shrugged. "You even do them on a Monday night."

His eyes flickered. "Pretty cool, huh?"

I laughed. "No wonder this is your dream job. You get paid to be a kid and have fun."

Patrick's smile widened. "That's because I'm Peter Pan, baby."

* * * *

Two days later, Patrick and I took the group snorkeling. This was the calmest activity the men had done all trip, and the first time the women joined us. Patrick and Tom were exhausted from all the action, so I volunteered to take Tom's place. This was also the first activity I could participate in.

Katie came in the galley while I packed bottles of water and sandwiches in the cooler bag. "Thanks, Victoria." She glowed with excitement.

"For what?"

"This is the first time Tom and I will be alone for days."

I laughed, knowing how she felt. "Enjoy it. It won't last long."

"I know. I'm going to."

She was still beaming when Tom trudged into the galley. "I'm going to bed." He grabbed a banana from the bowl as he headed downstairs. "Katie, wake me up when the boat returns."

Katie stood in the galley speechless. The light left her face. I smiled at her sympathetically. She broke into tears and fled the room.

* * * *

As we back-rolled off the tender into the water, all I saw was blue, as clear as glacier water, yet warm as sun-brewed tea. Rays of sunlight slanted down from above, illuminating the theater below us.

The women and I swam lazily, enjoying the scenery while the men searched for lobster. I swam with a mesh bag looped around my wrist to collect their catch. We snorkeled over a coral outcrop, fifteen feet below us. It was close enough to the surface for the women and I to explore, yet the bottom was deep enough to make it slightly more challenging for the men. I took pleasure being in the water instead of the galley for a change. An electric blue and blazing-yellow queen angel glided below us. A school of sergeant majors passed in a flurry of white, yellow and black stripes. The wives swam behind a purple sea fan and posed while I took their picture behind its veil.

We'd been snorkeling for about fifteen minutes when I spotted antennae sticking out from under a crop of coral. They sat too far underwater for me to get. I signaled to Patrick who wasn't far away, and he motioned for the CEO. Directly below him were three large lobsters, swaying back and forth in the swell.

The CEO nodded. He pinched his nose to clear his ears and dove down. With his gloved hand, he grabbed the body of the first lobster before it had time to scurry away. He curved his body and fluttered up to the surface where he spit the snorkel out of his mouth. "That's one." He swam over to me and placed the crustacean inside the bag.

"Well done," I said.

He lowered his mask over his eyes and replied, "I'm not done yet."

He popped his snorkel back in his mouth and disappeared underwater again. This time, he ascended with the other two lobsters, one in each hand. Patrick placed a gloved hand over the tail of one to steady it as he took it from the CEO. He placed it in the mesh bag and turned back to the man. "That'll be a nice appetizer tonight."

"Appetizer?" The man laughed. "They'll be our dinner. I'll go get three more."

You couldn't say he lacked confidence. The CEO dove down again while we all watched from the surface. True to his word, within ten minutes he had procured three more lobsters.

I couldn't help but be impressed. *Was there anything he couldn't do?*

We returned to the yacht, twenty minutes later, with six lobsters; one for each guest. Katie greeted us on the aft deck with a tray of champagne. Her eyes were red-rimmed, but I didn't think anyone would notice.

"To victory!" The men cheered and raised their glasses high.

Patrick leaned back on the railing, his face relaxed and happy. These were the moments he loved about yachting. His guests were enjoying themselves, and he had shown them a good time.

As Tom began rinsing the gear, Katie whispered. "There's something wrong with the air-conditioning." She looked over her shoulder to make sure the guests couldn't hear. "The boat's really hot."

And, just like that, the moment passed and Patrick was brought down to reality. Like a fickle mistress: the boat needed attention. Brow furrowed, he excused himself to go check the engine room. I followed in case he needed a second set of hands.

Katie and Tom entertained everyone on the aft as long as they could while Patrick primed the pump for the air-conditioner. He'd been forced to do the same thing a dozen times so far this trip.

"I don't know if this system will last much longer." He shook his head. "It's pretty old."

"Can we make it through the season?" I knew too little about engineering to offer any help.

He looked up, exasperated. "I don't know if it'll make it through this trip."

* * * *

The boat began to cool slowly, but it was unbearable to be inside until the system caught up. The hot tropical sun streamed through the pane glass windows and baked the interior. It felt like an oven when I walked through the doors.

I could hear Patrick on the phone with the manager. "This has to be our last trip," he said. "I need to get to a shipyard and get things fixed."

There was a pause while, I assumed, the manager spoke.

"We may not make it that long." He sighed. "The air-conditioner's broken, we need to run new pipes to the water heaters, and the radars are only bandaged together. We can't have guests like this." The frustration was rising in his voice.

Another long pause.

"Okay, we're coming home after this trip."

I sighed. The boat gave us trouble, but I liked being in the islands. I wasn't sure I wanted to go back to Florida and sit in a shipyard.

Patrick hung up and walked outside. I followed him, hoping to take his mind off the problems. The air hung heavy and didn't move. Patrick stood sullen, both hands on the cap-rail, staring out over the flat calm water.

"You know what today is?" I rubbed between his shoulder blades.

"The day I get fired?" Patrick sulked.

"No." I massaged his tight muscles. "It's our anniversary."

Patrick didn't say anything. He just stared ahead.

"Maybe we could go back to Anguilla to celebrate." I thought a short getaway from the boat would help Patrick's stress, and what better place to escape to than the island where we were married?

Patrick's head whipped around. He glared at me. Not out of surprise at the date like most husbands, but with irritation. "Yeah, laying on the beach for a week will make everything just peachy." He scowled. "Great idea, Victoria."

I reached up to scratch his head like he liked. "If the boat goes back to Lauderdale, maybe we can slip away for a weekend?"

He yanked his head out of my reach. "If we go back to Lauderdale, there's a good chance we'll be looking for a new job!"

I wasn't sure how to make him feel better. We encountered plenty of problems on the boat, but the guests had all been happy. "Well, then we can go to Anguilla for longer." I thought a joke might break the tension.

"What? No!" he spat. "Look, I can't deal with this now."

My eyes narrowed. "Deal with what?" My voice became squeaky. I was just trying to help. I hated when he took his frustration with the boat out on me. "Deal with me?"

"Not now, Victoria." he scoffed at me. "It's not all about you, you know."

I clenched my jaw. My body temperature spiked. *When had it ever been all about me?* My nails dug into my palms as I tightened my hands into fists. *Did he think we were on this sinking ship because I wanted to be?* I opened my mouth and started to tell Patrick just what I thought when the CEO came around the corner.

My mouth snapped shut. I plastered a smile on my face. "Hello, sir."

"Captain, we'll leave for the airport tomorrow at noon." He glanced at his phone and turned to me. "We'll take a packed lunch. There's a microwave onboard the jet, but no oven, so make it sandwiches and salads."

I nodded and forced a smile. "Certainly."

While I listened to Patrick and the man talk about the logistics of getting them to the airport, my mind seethed. *I couldn't even have a fight with my husband on this boat.* As soon as the man left, I stormed back to the galley. Patrick called after me, but I pretended I couldn't hear him and left him standing on the side deck.

I took my anger out on my chopping block. I slammed two carrots on its surface and raised my chef's knife like a cleaver. I hacked at the vegetables with a force I didn't know I possessed. Whack! Whack! Whack! The blade repeatedly went straight through the root and struck the surface of the wood. Chunks of orange sprayed across the galley. On the last chop, the knife embedded in the block and stuck. I stepped back and ran my hands through my hair, grabbing tight and pulling until my scalp lifted. "Ugh!"

"Everything okay?" Katie asked from the doorway.

I looked at the mess I made and the scared look on Katie's face. "Yeah, I just... I..." I couldn't form my anger into words. "Boys!" I blew out the word and felt the anger ease with it. I laughed.

Katie laughed too. "I know!"

* * * *

Patrick stayed in the bridge, avoiding the galley. I had calmed down a little, but I couldn't stop thinking about what he'd said. Where he had the ability to fight and forget about it ten minutes later, I tended to hold onto my anger for days. It boiled inside me. I could hold a grudge forever and knew this particular blow-up was far from resolved.

I stewed while I peeled and diced the potatoes for a salad and thought about my options. I could refuse to cook his dinner until he apologized. He would go awful hungry without me making his eggs in the morning. I chopped capers as I decided that was too tame a punishment.

I could put peas in every meal I made for the next week. He hated them and would go crazy with frustration. Too childish, I figured.

I picked up a bunch of jade green parsley. I could quit. I could swim to shore and hop the next flight off the island. That would teach him. Let him try and explain to the CEO he was trying so hard to impress why the chef, his wife, wasn't on board to cook his dinner. I chewed on the side of my lip. That wasn't really a good plan. Where would I go? Back to our house and wait for him there?

No, I was stuck. I had no recourse. I would just have to be mad and wait for it to go away. There is no revenge when your husband is also your boss.

But, whether I was mad or not, I still had a dinner to cook. I was about to start on the lobster when the CEO stuck his head in the galley. "I just wanted to see how our friends were doing." *Friends?* That wasn't a good sign. He was bonding with our dinner.

His wife followed behind him. "Oh, there they are." She stopped short and raised her hand to cover her mouth. "Ohh!" She suddenly realized what was about to happen. Her eyes widened. Her voice became shrill. "What are you going to do with them?'

The rest of the guests joined the couple in the galley. All watched wide-eyed and awaited my answer. "We're going to have a feast." I smiled brightly, hoping a festive mood would distract them from what I was about to do. I had made a cake earlier to celebrate the man's birthday. I hoped I could distract them with the party. "A celebration for your last night."

"Our lobster is a great way to celebrate," one man agreed.

I picked up my knife and hesitated before commencing the next step in my recipe. This wasn't something guests normally liked to see. But there they were, standing in the galley watching me. I was about to kill a lobster. I raised my weapon. As I held on to its spiny body with my left hand, the lobster bucked like a bull and wiggled free. He scurried across the cutting board. I made a grab for him and slid him back into place. I smiled sheepishly and picked up my knife again, but the affect was not lost on the guests. I was about to murder their dinner.

"Don't you just boil them or something?" the CEO's wife asked.

"Actually, boiling water takes longer for them to die." As soon as the words were out of my mouth I regretted them. I really didn't want to be discussing the death of their dinner with them. "The knife pierces their brain and kills them instantly." *Did I just say that?* "This is more humane."

My smile was met with looks of disbelief.

"Oh, I can't watch!" The squeamish wife turned on her heel and left. The others stayed. It was their lobster after all.

All eyes shifted to me. I placed the tip of my knife between the lobster's body and its head and pushed down, splitting it in two. Crack! The sound of its shell shattering rang through the galley. A viscous grey-green liquid oozed out of the head cavity. The second woman turned her back and shuddered.

"I'll be on the aft deck if you need me," she said to her husband.

Everyone but the CEO silently filed out the door.

"Sorry," I muttered. I kept my head down, afraid to see the horror in his eyes. I didn't mean to be terrorizing the guests. I was supposed to be showing them a good time.

I twisted the lobster's body from its head. My head darted up as I stole a glance at the man to see how he was taking the display. I saw him wince. I was surprised. He looked as green as the parsley. I separated the delicate flesh of the lobster from the shell. He swallowed hard.

I was confused. *Wasn't he the tough guy? How did he think food got to his plate in the first place? Was he one of those people who believed chicken breasts came from the grocery store already packaged and didn't put any thought into how it got there?* I looked up from my cutting board and caught his eye.

He squared his shoulders. "I think we'll have grilled cheese sandwiches." He headed for the door, leaving the scene of the massacre. He stopped short and added, "I think, my friends would prefer that."

I hung my head. Today was not a good day. This wasn't the end to our first season and our first year of marriage that I'd been hoping for.

———— VICTORIA ALLMAN ————

Pan-Seared Grouper
with Thai Curry Sauce

Paste:

1 teaspoon sambal olek
1 teaspoon sea salt
1 tablespoon fresh galangal, grated (or from a jar)
2 tablespoons chopped lemongrass
1 tablespoon ground coriander
1 teaspoon turmeric
2 shallots, rough chopped
6 cloves garlic, rough chopped
1 tablespoon shrimp paste
1/2 teaspoon white pepper
1 teaspoon cumin
3 lime leaves, chopped fine
2 tablespoons cilantro, rough chopped
2 tablespoons Thai basil, rough chopped (you can use regular basil if Thai variety is not available)

Sauce:

2 tablespoons canola oil
1 tablespoon palm sugar
2 tablespoons fish sauce
2 cans coconut milk
2 limes, juiced

Grouper:

6 six-ounce pieces grouper
1 teaspoon sea salt
1/4 teaspoon white pepper
1/4 cup cornstarch
1/4 cup canola oil

Place all the ingredients for the paste in a food processor and process until a smooth paste is formed.

In a heavy-bottomed pot, heat canola oil over medium-high heat. Add the paste and fry for three minutes, stirring constantly to release aroma of the paste. Add the palm sugar and stir for 20 seconds. Add fish sauce and stir another 20 seconds. Add the coconut milk. Bring to a boil, reduce heat and simmer for 10 minutes. Taste and add lime juice for acidity, sugar for sweetness, fish sauce for salt, or sambal olek for heat to your preference.

Preheat oven to 350 degrees.

~Continued on next page

Season fish with sea salt and white pepper. Dust with cornstarch. Heat a heavy-bottomed skillet over high heat. Add the canola oil and sear the fish on each side for 2 minutes until golden. Place on a cookie sheet and roast in the oven for 5 more minutes.

While fish is cooking, place sauce in a blender and puree. Strain.

Serve fish on a bed of rice with sauce and a stir-fry of: zucchini, carrots, red onions, snap peas and red peppers.

Serves 6

Warm Lobster Potato Salad

Lobster Tails:
6 lobsters
1/4 cup olive oil
4 cloves garlic
1 onion, rough chop
1/2 cup brandy
12 cups water
2 carrots, peeled and rough chop
2 stalks celery, rough chop
1 tomato, rough chop
1 teaspoon sea salt
1 teaspoon black peppercorns
6 sprigs parsley

Mayonnaise:
1 egg yolk
1/4 teaspoon sea salt
8 grinds of black pepper
1 teaspoon Dijon mustard
1 lemon, juiced
1 tablespoon white wine vinegar
3/4 cup canola oil

Warm Potato Salad:
6 waxy potatoes (6 cups)
1/2 cup green onions, finely chopped
2 tablespoons parsley, finely chopped
2 tablespoons capers
2 tablespoons gherkins, finely chopped
2 roasted red peppers, diced into $\frac{1}{4}$" cubes
1 cup peas
1 lemon, juiced
1 teaspoon sea salt

~Continued on next page

For the lobsters:
Kill the lobsters by using a heavy chef's knife to cut through their head, between their eyes (This kills their brain instantly and is the most humane way). Twist their bodies from their tails, reserving the heads for the stock.

Using heavy kitchen shears, cut down the bellies of the lobster tails and remove the meat from the shell. Pull the black vein from inside the top of the meat to remove. Place the meat in the fridge for later use. Cut the hard shells into pieces.

In a heavy bottomed pot, sauté the garlic and the onion in $\frac{1}{4}$ cup olive oil for two minutes over medium-high heat until just soft. Add the lobster shells and heads and stir until they turn coral pink. Deglaze the pan with brandy. Add the water, carrots, celery, tomato, sea salt, black pepper and parsley. When the stock starts to boil turn the burner to medium-low and simmer for 20 minutes.

Strain the stock and reserve the liquid.

Bring the stock to a gentle simmer. Add the lobster tails and reduce heat to medium-low. Poach the tails for 6 minutes. Set tails aside to cool. Save the stock for soups, sauces, or poaching fish.

Slice the lobster tails in coins.

For the mayonnaise:
Place the yolk, sea salt, black pepper, Dijon mustard, lemon juice, and white wine vinegar in the bowl of a food processor fitted with the metal chopping blade. With the motor running slowly drizzle in canola oil, no faster than a fine stream until all of the oil is incorporated.

For the potato salad:
Peel and dice potatoes into 1-inch cubes. Boil in salted water until tender. Drain and cool.

In the meantime, boil the peas in salted water for 2 minutes. Drain.

Mix the lobster, potatoes, peas, green onions, parsley, capers, gherkins and roasted red peppers. Gently toss together with mayonnaise, lemon juice and sea salt. Taste for seasoning and serve.

Serves 6

A Change of Scenery

I stayed in the galley that night longer than normal. After the lobster debacle, I rearranged the spices in my drawer and used the dust buster to suck out the flour in the corners of the baking cupboard. I avoided our cabin until I was sure Patrick would be asleep. Finally, I ran out of jobs to waste time. I descended the stairs and crept through the cabin door. Patrick lay on top of the bed, curled in a fetal position, still in his uniform. He looked peaceful and stress-free. A new wave of frustration washed over me and my anger boiled again. I slammed the cabin door and hit the light switch. Bright light flooded the room.

Patrick raised his hand to shield his eyes and squinted. "Have the guests gone to bed?" he mumbled.

I ignored him and went into the bathroom. By the time I came out, he was under the covers and asleep again. I climbed into bed, careful not to touch him, and lay staring at the ceiling. *You're being childish. He's just stressed.* The minutes ticked by. Like a cradle, the dark room rocked back and forth with the swell. I replayed the idea of swimming to shore again and again in my mind.

The alarm rang at five and I stumbled out of bed. Patrick lay in the exact same position he'd been in the night before.

The morning was quiet. As I baked muffins and lemon coconut squares for the guests to take on the plane, the sky turned from blueberry to blue suede.

Spikes of light shot skyward behind a fluffy white cloud lined with silver. No one was around to see it. I stood outside the galley door, sipping my coffee and watching the sunrise. A pure white sea bird soared overhead. It circled once before changing direction and plunging straight down. It disappeared into the water, leaving only a ring in the water to verify its existence. A moment later, the bird resurfaced, carrying a small ballyhoo in its beak. He flew off toward the island and all was quiet again. *Why wasn't every morning like this?*

Slowly, the boat began to wake. Tom began chamoixing the aft deck and uncovering the chairs. Katie dusted and vacuumed the main salon. The CEO appeared in shorts and a Nike t-shirt and jumped onto the treadmill. Patrick still hadn't come upstairs. I looked at my watch and rolled my eyes. Whether I was avoiding him or not, it was time for him to get up and start the engines so we could get back to the dock in time for the guest's to catch their plane.

I climbed downstairs and called from the doorway. "Patrick." My voice was icy. The lump in the bed didn't move. "Patrick!" I yelled louder. "It's time to get up." No response. "Patrick!" I screamed this time. Nothing.

I huffed, my anger resurfacing again. I stormed over to the bed and whipped the duvet off his sleeping shape. My fiery glare was met with soft Egyptian cotton. In place of Patrick's body were three beige pillows contorted and wrinkled into a curve. I was confused. I stood staring, not able to comprehend what I was seeing. *Did he swim to shore?*

From behind me, I heard a giggle. I whipped around to see Patrick hiding behind the bathroom door, his shoulders shaking in laughter. He brought his hand up to his mouth and bobbed his head in an exaggerated chuckle. His periwinkle eyes lit with mischief.

I picked up one of the pillows from his ruse and hurled it at him. He ducked and it sailed over his head into the door. "Ha, ha!" His voice sounded like a fifth grade smart aleck's.

I turned and grabbed the remaining pillows with both hands and threw them one after the other at his head. The first one struck his shoulder, knocking him slightly off balance. The second was a direct hit. His head bounced back and hit the bathroom door with a dull thud. He stood dazed for a moment, then lowered his head and growled, charging like a bull. He caught me around the waist and threw me to the bed. He jumped on top of me and straddled my waist. "Ha, ha!" he growled menacingly.

I couldn't hold it in any more. "Agh!" I exploded and kicked my arms and legs trying to wiggle free.

Patrick held tight. "Ha ha," he said even more maniacally and then began to laugh.

I couldn't help it. I started to laugh too. I laughed hard. Tears ran down the side of my face. I couldn't stop. I gasped for air. "Get off me!"

Patrick rolled to the side and headed for the bathroom. "See, you can't stay mad at me forever."

* * * *

The morning flew past and the guests left for the airport. We packed the boat and latched all cupboards and doors. Tom tied the outside chairs to the table and we taped all the hatches. None of us wanted a repeat of the rough seas of our trip getting here.

"Ready?" Patrick asked when all was secure.

"Ready." Tom nodded.

"Okay, let's go get this tub fixed."

And with that, we headed back to Lauderdale. We pulled into the shipyard a week later and immediately went about tearing apart the engine room. Contractors arrived daily at seven and hammered and clanged all day long. The old water-maker came out and a new one went in. The air-conditioner compressor was replaced and a tech came by to reset the radars. Katie and I shopped for new dishes and Tom was able to take his advanced firefighting class. We were a quarter of the way through the project when the manager called us into his office.

"What do you think he wants?" Patrick was nervous; his job was far from guaranteed. And, now here we were spending a lot of the owner's money on repairs.

"Don't worry," I told him as he fidgeted with the collar on his polo. "We'll be fine."

"It's only been six months," Patrick fretted. "And we had all those damages."

"Well, technically, only a few were our fault." It was a lame excuse and I knew it.

"I don't want to get fired from my first position as captain."

I tried to make a joke. "You can always say it was your wife's fault."

Patrick looked at me without laughing. "Don't think I won't."

I hoped he was joking too.

We entered the bright white building and passed framed photos of mega yachts anchored in Corsica, Australia, and St. Lucia, each one bigger than the last, hanging in the hallway. The manager's office was the last door we came to. By then, Patrick had beads of sweat below his hairline.

He turned to me as he reached for the door handle. "Ready?"

"Whatever happens, we're in this together."

He smiled briefly and turned the handle.

The manager sat behind his desk talking on his iPhone. He waved us in and motioned for us to sit. He kept talking, giving me a chance to look around and Patrick a chance to become more nervous. The man's desk was covered in boat brochures and yachting magazines. His Tommy Bahamas silk shirt looked perfectly pressed, along with his khaki linen pants.

"I'll fly in to Athens in the morning," he said. "We can sign the contracts then." He hung up and shone a bright smile at us.

"So, tell me guys. How do you like the boat?"

"Well," Patrick started. "We had a few problems to begin with, but now..."

The manager shuffled some papers on his desk, not seeming to pay much attention to what Patrick was saying.

"The reason I ask is that one of my clients in Europe is looking for a new crew on his charter boat."

The lines of worry on Patrick's face smoothed like icing under my spatula.

"I think you two would be perfect."

Patrick was trying to suppress a smile and sound professional. "Well, I wouldn't want to leave this boat in the lurch."

The manager waved his hand as if dismissing the notion as preposterous. "I have someone who could take over the yard period." He shuffled more papers. "Besides, you and I both know that boat will be in there for a long time."

It was true. Fixing the pipes was going to be a major undertaking. The boat would probably be out of commission for the upcoming summer season. I tried not to get too excited. As a chef, Europe was a dream come true. I bit my lip and looked at Patrick. He was trying to stop the corners of his mouth from curling up.

"Bigger boat?"

"Yep, in good condition."

"Needs all new crew?"

"The owner just bought a new boat and the old crew is moving onto it." The manager nodded. "The old boat is being used strictly for charter." He handed me a brochure with a large white yacht on the cover. It had three levels of decks, which was one more than we had now, and looked to be eighty-feet longer.

I flipped through the pages, past pictures of the steam room onboard, a gym, and luxurious master stateroom, to the galley. I gasped. Shining from the glossy page, a stainless sub-zero refrigerator, Viking range, and granite countertop caught my eye. The space was massive. A walk-in fridge and freezer were listed on the side of the page as well as an indoor grill and built-in wok.

I handed the brochure to Patrick. "Nice." I whistled.

He turned to the specs of the bridge. "Brand new radars, depth sounders, and chart plotters. Impressive." He nodded.

I pointed to a door off the bridge. "What's that?"

The manager looked up from his iPhone. "That's your cabin."

"Upstairs? Away from the crew?"

He nodded. On this boat, the captain would need to be close to the bridge so he could be available if something went wrong. We would be separated from everyone else and practically living on our own. My smile widened.

"Europe?" Patrick asked.

Another nod. "Starts in Genoa, then trips already booked for Cannes, St. Tropez, Greece, Spain."

Patrick's smile widened, too. "Count us in!"

* * * *

"What do you guys think about joining us in Europe?" Patrick asked Tom and Katie the next day at lunch. I was already excited and had roasted a pork loin for *porchetta* and stewed vegetables for *ratatouille* to practice my Mediterranean recipes.

Tom's smile confirmed his love of the job while Katie's betrayed her lack of enthusiasm. "Really?" Tom asked. "You'd want us on the new boat?"

"Of course." Patrick reached for a slice of fresh mozzarella while he spoke. "You've done a great job."

Tom agreed right away. "That'd be awesome."

Katie dropped her eyes and avoided looking Patrick in the eye. "Maybe we should talk about it and get back to you tomorrow."

Tom looked at her, perplexed, but I knew what she meant. This wasn't the life for her.

* * * *

Two weeks later, we jumped on a plane and landed in Italy. Patrick had talked to both Tom and Katie. Tom wanted to come with us, but since Katie refused to sign on again, he felt he should stay with Katie. He was going to enroll in captain's classes; he was hooked on this lifestyle and wanted to start his training. Katie had hinted at the fact she was going to return to school, but really she didn't want another yachting job.

She hadn't taken to yachting with as much enthusiasm. The life was hard for women. For a few years, the travel and money were exciting, but eventually one got tired of cleaning up after other people. She wanted kids and a house she could decorate, maybe a garden to play in. Those things didn't work with yachting.

It would be easier on Tom, who could follow this path to the top; becoming a captain and travel the world. It could be a career for him, but for Katie, this was a limited time period. We would miss them. They were fun to be around. Living in such close quarters, one grows either close with others or very, very angry. We were lucky we all liked each other and got along well.

Patrick and I arrived in Genoa, tired and worn from a long day on the plane. We lugged our bags, heavy with everything we would need for the next year on the new boat, down narrow streets to the busy port. Frustrated by lack of taxis and grumpy from empty, growling stomachs, we stopped at the first restaurant we came to.

It was nothing special, just a few plastic patio tables and chairs overlooking the commercial port. A laminated menu translated a handful of pizzas and half a dozen pastas into a comical form of English. *Smelly Blue Cheese seated on Linguini* was the one that made me smile. But, I opted for a simple dish of pesto pasta I ordered with *Drink Water* and a carafe of wine. I was too tired to try and think of anything more exciting.

We raised our glasses of Chianti in a toast.

"To the next chapter." I held my glass high. The warm Mediterranean breeze blew off the harbor. A starlit sky sparkled above.

"The next chapter," he agreed and clinked glasses with me.

When my dish arrived, I was surprised by the color. When I made pesto, the paste was dark green. Mine was strong and bit with the licorice-taste of basil. This, in front of me, was creamier and a softer green. I took a bite. It was not as sharp as my version. It was rich in flavor, but smooth and well balanced. With each bite, a taste of what I could only describe as green, filled my senses.

"Mmm," was all I could say. Patrick barely acknowledged me. He was too busy devouring his own plate of thin noodles with calamari, mussels, and scampi. Golden slivers of fried garlic decorated the top of his dish. It was disappearing as quickly as mine.

I ate the bright green pasta with wonder and relished each bite. This is what being in Europe was going to be like, discovering new tastes, finding new recipes.

The next morning I danced on my toes, excited to go discover the secrets of that dish. Patrick stayed behind in the hotel room to arrange a time to board the new boat. We were to meet the departing captain and crew and have a one-week handover of information before they flew to Germany and Patrick took over.

Patrick had set up a makeshift desk on the bed and was talking on the phone. His Italian dictionary was open in front of him and he flipped its pages like shuffling cards.

"*Barca*," he shouted in hopes the loudness of his voice would make up for his butchered accent. "*Dove?*"

I would be no help to him. French I could stumble through, but Italian was a mystery to me. I could say hello and list a few food words, but past that I was lost. I felt for Patrick, having to stumble through a business conversation in a foreign language.

I headed for the market, where all good food discoveries begin. Leaving the seaport, I climbed winding cobblestone streets through the medieval old town past pastry shops, cafes, and palazzos. I followed narrow alleyways and wandered down wide streets, my attention swinging back and forth to the ancient buildings and shops until I got to via XX Settembre.

When I entered the covered market, I was accosted by smells and sounds exploding around me. The warm smell of *focaccia* baking in one stall mingled with the salty smell of the sea from tables of fish and seafood. Italian men in stretched and misshapen white tank tops called out their greetings to me.

"*Buongiorno*," I replied, trying out the few words of Italian I knew. "*Basilico?*" I raised my eyebrow, hoping they would understand.

"*Si, si.*" A man waved me over, wearing no more than a white apron over his faded baby blue boxers and the bright orange clogs that Mario Batali made famous. He handed me a bunch of small-leafed, emerald-green basil. The tiny delicate leaves meant the plant could be no more than a few days old. He broke off the heart of a stem and rubbed the leaves between his thick rough fingers. He brought them to his face and breathed deeply, shutting his eyes and smiling. He was lost in sensation. He opened his eyes in a dreamy, lulled way and broke into an Italian soliloquy for the next three minutes. I didn't understand a word he said, but his voice sounded like music. I smiled and nodded.

Maybe he knew I didn't understand him. Instead of repeating, he cupped his hand gently behind my head and held the basil out for me to smell. It was a sensual act. I leaned in, closed my eyes and took a deep breath. The aroma nudged my memory.

This was different from the basil I had known. It smelled sweet and mellow. I smiled with the same hazy look he had.

"*Due.*" I held up two fingers to make sure he knew what I wanted. As I walked away in search of the Parmesan and pine nuts I needed to complete my dish, the man broke into song. His deep baritone voice reverberated like opera through the market.

No wonder the pasta the night before tasted so good. In Italy, there is life and love in everything.

Porchetta

1 tablespoon fennel seeds
1 tablespoon coarse sea salt
24 grinds black pepper
1 teaspoon crushed red pepper
2 branches of rosemary, chopped
6 cloves garlic. minced
1/4 cup olive oil
4 pounds boneless center-cut pork loin
1 teaspoon sea salt

The Day Before:
In a spice grinder, process fennel seeds, sea salt, pepper and crushed peppers. In a large bowl, mix ground spices, rosemary, garlic and olive oil. Rub on pork loin and marinate in the fridge for 24 hours.

The Next Day:
Preheat oven to 400 degrees.
Place pork, fat side up in a roasting pan. Sprinkle the last teaspoon of sea salt over the pork. Roast for 10 minutes at 400 degrees and then lower oven to 300 degrees for 30 minutes until the center of the loin registers 140 degrees on a meat thermometer. Let pork loin rest for 20 minutes. Slice into quarter-inch thick slices and arrange on a platter.

Serves 8

Pesto

2 cloves garlic, minced
1/2 teaspoon sea salt
2 cups fresh basil leaves, packed tight (4 ounces in weight)
3 tablespoons pine nuts
1/2 cup Parmesan, grated
1/2 cup olive oil

In a heavy bottomed frying pan, sauté the pine nuts over medium heat. Shake the pan constantly so they do not burn. Toast until they turn golden. Remove from heat and cool.

To create the soft creamy pesto of Genoa, grind the garlic cloves and salt in a mortar and pestle (hence the name pesto). Add the basil leaves and press until a rough paste is achieved. Add the pine nuts and Parmesan and press to incorporate. Slowly add the olive oil to emulsify into the mix.

You can also use a food processor for larger batches, but the blades will bruise the basil leaves and the color will darken.

If not using right away, place in an airtight container and cover with 2 tablespoons olive oil to prevent the air from oxidizing the pesto.

When using pesto for pasta, dilute it with half a cup of the pasta cooking water, after the pasta is cooked. This will make the pesto 'saucier' so it will coat the noodles.

Makes 2 cups pesto

Normal Hours

*U*ntil then, I'd been lucky. During the past nine years of yachting, I'd worked *normal* hours. Of course, I'm not talking nine to five, Monday to Friday, but a regular schedule of up at five-thirty to begin the day's baking and finished by ten—eleven at the latest. Some trips slid earlier or slightly later as guests relaxed into their vacation schedule. But my life on yachts had been a consistent schedule. I considered these normal hours … until the Cannes charter began.

This was our first trip of the season and our maiden voyage on the new boat. When we arrived in Italy, Patrick's main concern was putting together a strong crew. He needed to hire seven new faces. As soon as we were onboard, he made calls to people we knew, but everyone already had a job for the summer. We would be starting fresh. In between learning the boat and moving aboard, he interviewed dozens of candidates. He met with four people in the morning and four in the afternoon. This went on for days while I scrubbed floors, sorted through uniforms, and organized cupboards. Each day, Patrick would offer one or two of the people a position and they would arrive, bags in hand, the next day. Chloe, the chief stew from New Zealand started first, then Stoyan, our Bulgarian engineer. Nick from England, Dylan from Ireland, and Todd from Australia followed. And, finally, Gwen from Sweden and Anna from Croatia completed the new hires. We had a team.

"I like the idea of hiring an international crew," Patrick said at dinner the next night. "There'll be lots of new stories to talk about."

"Things won't be boring," I agreed. "That's for sure." I should have known that would be an understatement.

The boat kept us busy. We had two weeks to pull everything together, get to know one another, and sort out our departments.

"Why is there never enough time?" Patrick stood in the wheelhouse surrounded by paperwork. "There's a week of stuff to do and we have to move the boat to France…" he looked at his watch, "in two days."

I stood behind him and wrapped my arms around his waist. "We'll get there." I said. "It always feels like this. And, we always pull it together."

He untangled himself from my grasp, not wanting solace. "That doesn't make this any easier. There's still a ton of work to do." He sighed with the exaggeration of Zsa Zsa Gabor. Some days he could be so dramatic.

"How about I go pick up some of that fresh linguini we had the other night and make *vongoli* for lunch?"

The right corner of his pursed lips curled skyward and his eyes, the color of Snow White's dress, sparkled to life. "With some of the *focaccia* from this morning?" And with that, the stress flowed away like pouring orange juice down the sink.

* * * *

And, pull it together we did. We all did what we knew had to be done, and on Wednesday, Patrick slid the new boat off the dock for the first time.

"All lines are clear," Nick, our new first mate called on the radio from the aft deck.

"The channel is clear," the bosun, Dylan's Irish accent, called next.

On this larger boat with more crew, I was no longer needed to help with lines and fenders. Patrick breathed easier knowing trained hands were on deck who knew what they were doing. We pulled out of port and waved goodbye to the latest in a string of new places we would explore.

That afternoon I stood on deck watching while we pulled into Old Port Cannes without incident. As the deck crew set the fenders, Patrick walked around the decks to inspect the docking and our position. His smile said it all. He spoke into his radio, "Great job, guys." To me he said, "We're back."

I didn't understand. We'd never been to Cannes before.

He waved his arm to indicate the new boat around him. The outside had been polished the day before by Todd, the deckhand, and the paint shone. Dylan had scrubbed the teak decks until they looked brand new. The boat had responded properly at sea and not one alarm went off while we traveled.

Patrick beamed as bright as our mast light. "This is the boat for us."

* * * *

The charter was to begin the next day, and began as all the others had. The twelve guests arrived at one o'clock. The crew stood on the aft deck lined up like chess pieces to meet them. Chloe, our new chief stew, held a tray of champagne flutes while Gwen, the second stewardess, offered hors d'oerves. Anna, our junior stewardess, waited to help with luggage and unpack their bags. We greeted the guests with all the flash both the yacht and the town had to offer and the guests glittered back. They were young, beautiful people from Rio.

As Chloe spoke with the principal about their plans, I headed back to the galley to plate the Salad Niçoise and Parmesan-crusted Chicken for lunch. It was a light meal that reflected the Provençal countryside surrounding us.

The new galley was a dream. Now, I had two ovens for baking, eight induction burners for fast cooking, and an indoor grill. The floor was bamboo hardwood and the marble counter tops where I stood to work looked out over three large picture windows. I would have an amazing view of passing scenery as I cooked.

As I tossed arugula in lemon and olive oil, I couldn't help but smile, because I was back to cooking in a proper, high-quality kitchen. This was a space where I wouldn't need to compromise or cut corners because of limited equipment.

Chloe returned, not with a time for lunch, but with orders for omelets. "They'd like a basket of toast and croissants and a platter of meats and cheeses." She laughed, knowing what breakfast at two in the afternoon meant. Her dark hair and green eyes gave her an exotic look that molded into stunning when she smiled.

I rolled my eyes. "Are you ready for this?"

She shrugged. "I'll have to be." And, with that, she was gone, out to the cupboard to pull the napkins and placemats.

I smiled to myself. I liked her. She was quick, efficient, and knew what had to be done. On this boat, I would be able to concentrate on cooking instead of worrying about service and cleaning as well. I breathed a sigh of relief and quickly began slicing fruit and pulling yogurts out of the fridge.

By four-thirty we had served breakfast and cleared. It went flawlessly; not a drop spilled or a plate broken. I wiped the counter and began to sweep.

Chloe grabbed the broom out of my hand. "I'll do that."

I amended my earlier thought; I loved this chief stew.

I looked at my watch and panicked. I was late to start cooking crew dinner. I busied myself by chopping green onions for *kung pao* shrimp and sausage for fried rice. I shredded some of the untouched chicken from the first guest lunch I made for Dylan, who was allergic to shellfish, and ran down the ingredient list to make sure the rest of the crew could eat everything. Although they were always the ones to be flexible when guests were aboard, I tried to feed the crew what they liked to eat and keep to a regular schedule of lunch at noon and dinner at six. They gave up enough control of their lives in never being able to plan what they were doing or where they were headed, and I felt the least I could do was make their meals as normal and enjoyable as possible.

I stripped the shrimp of their protective shells and scattered them in a hot pan to sear. I sprinkled slivers of garlic over them and circled a wooden spoon around the pan to prevent burning and sticking. This was instinctual. I paid attention to what I was doing, but I could do it fast and efficiently. Repetition of recipes had given me the confidence to let my mind wander while I cooked. *What would this new boat be like? Could we call our cabin home for awhile?* The galley was quiet while I worked. The rest of the crew were busy in their own departments. I treasured these solitary times in the galley, but knew they wouldn't last.

Chloe returned at five to inform me the guests were napping. "They would like platters of tomato and mozzarella, one of *bresaola* and one of melon and prosciutto, when they wake up." It sounded a lot like a lunch to me. I looked at my watch and wondered if this would be normal hours for the next ten days. Chloe shrugged. "We're in Europe, and meal times are a whole different thing over here."

I nodded and laughed. "Well, at least we'll have time during the day to head to the market."

"And the wine store," she added. "They've already drunk six bottles of *rosé* during lunch." She made quotation marks in the air with her fingers during the word lunch.

This was definitely going to be a different trip than the families and couples we had on the last boat.

Patrick was the next one through the door. "What's for dinner?" He picked up my wooden spoon and stirred the pan. After six years of cooking lunch and dinner for him, he was familiar with my repertoire and didn't need an answer. "Yum, my favorite."

"It'll be a few minutes late."

"You okay?" He rarely inquired about the galley, knowing I usually had it handled.

"Yep, lunch just ran a little late." I mimicked Chloe's air quotations. "This could be an interesting trip."

* * * *

At six-thirty I plated the salads and sliced the *focaccia* I had baked hours before. Chloe entered the galley. "There's talk of dinner later." She looked at her watch. "I guess maybe eleven o'clock?"

Starting dinner at eleven? Thoughts of getting to bed anytime remotely civilized washed away like the receding tide. "You better put on a pot of coffee."

"Already brewing."

Dinner did in fact start that late. Dressed in their Oscar de la Renta dresses and Dolce and Gabana shirts, the guests trickled onto the owner's deck by ten. The sun had already set and the lights of town twinkled on. A sultry breeze blew off the Mediterranean Sea, slightly cooling off the heat of the day. On the aft deck of the boats docked next to us, guests were already finishing their dinners.

I sent out hors d'ouerves of baked figs with *Roquefort* and spoons of salmon tartar. Our guests sipped champagne, lingered, and savored. They obviously knew one another well and had lots to talk about. No one seemed to be jumping up and moving to the dinner table any time soon. This was going to be a long night.

"They want another bottle of champagne before dinner." Chloe pulled more flutes from the cupboard. "Can you hold off for another half hour?"

"I'll send out another round of hors d'ouerves." I filled pastries with brie and roasted garlic.

"Something quick," Chloe encouraged. "I don't want this to go on all night."

Too late for that, I thought.

Gwen came in as Chloe was popping the cork on their third bottle. "Can I start turn-downs?"

Chloe looked at her watch. This was a job that normally was started at seven and finished by nine. Everyone's schedule was sliding. "Yes, if they go back for a nap now it better be for the night."

* * * *

Finally, dinner service started. Anna and Gwen had finished the cabins and Anna had been sent to bed. She would have to be up early to start laundry and set-up for breakfast. Gwen stayed on to help with service; she was the late girl.

Four courses and almost three hours later, I finished mopping the galley floor. I looked at the clock—two-fifteen. The guests had just left for Palais, the popular nightclub. Chloe disappeared after cleaning up dinner, and I was right behind her.

"Sleep well," was all I could manage to mumble as we went our separate ways. I stumbled to bed beside an already sleeping Patrick, resetting my five-fifteen alarm for later. There was no way the guests would be up early for breakfast.

I slept hard. It was the type of sleep where your body actually aches. My feet throbbed, my head pounded. There was a dull yet constant pulling in my lower back. I don't know how long I was curled up in my bunk when there came a soft tapping on my cabin door.

Gwen's Swedish accent floated across the room. "Um, Victoria."

Patrick jolted out of bed like a cannon shot. "What? What's wrong?" His blond hair stood straight on end. There was a wild look in his eyes while he tried to figure out what was happening. Late night wake-ups usually signaled a boat problem.

Gwen sounded terrified. "Sorry captain," her voice shook. "I just need Victoria."

"Oh, good." He fell back onto his pillow and was snoring before I had even responded.

"Uughrumph." I couldn't make my mouth form words.

"The guests just got home and would like something to eat," Gwen whispered.

"What time is it?" I jumped out of bed thinking I'd overslept. I searched the floor frantically for my uniform.

"Four-thirty."

I stiffened like egg whites for a meringue. "In the morning?"

Gwen nodded. Her eyes were wide, and she bit the bottom her lip. "I'm sorry, they asked me to wake you."

"No problem." I fumbled with my skort. "Always wake me. That's why we get paid the big bucks." I hoped I sounded more convincing than I felt. "I'll be down in a minute."

Gwen shut the door, and I stared at the uniform in my hand. *Should I wear the white one I had on two hours ago or grab tomorrow's blue one?* I was too confused to think. *Was this a new day yet, or not?* I threw on my wrinkled polo from dinner service and followed Gwen to the galley, trying to decide what type of meal people ate at four-thirty in the morning. *Breakfast or a late-night dinner? A snack or a meal?*

I groped the wall for the light switch and walked straight to the coffee machine, as Gwen lined up glasses for Patron. While the guests threw back the burning liquor, I set up my own shot. I tipped my head back and opened my throat for the jolt of caffeine that would get me through this.

Gwen returned and I immediately brewed two more shots. We held our espresso cups high and clinked in a toast. I shot a second round. My body shuddered involuntarily and my eyes squeezed shut. "This is going to be a long week."

Bresaola

1/2 pound bresaola, sliced thin
2 cups baby arugula
2 tablespoons Extra-Virgin Olive Oil
1/2 lemon, juiced
1/4 teaspoon sea salt
1/4 cup shaved Parmesan
4-5 grinds of fresh pepper

Arrange bresaola overlapping slightly in concentric circles on a platter. In a bowl mix together arugula, olive oil and sea salt. Toss gently. Pile on top of bresaola. With a vegetable peeler, shave ribbons of Parmesan onto platter. Grind fresh black pepper over salad.

Serves 4

Salmon Tartar

2 pounds Atlantic salmon
2 tablespoons finely chopped shallots
3 tablespoons chopped chives
1 tablespoon chopped capers
1 lemon, zested
3 tablespoons lemon juice
1 tablespoon olive oil
1 teaspoon sea salt
12 grinds fresh black pepper

~Continued on next page

Garnish:
Thin sliced cucumbers
Lemon Zest
Microgreens

Cut salmon into small dice with a sharp knife without mincing it. Refrigerate until ready to serve.

In a medium bowl, mix together the shallot, chives, capers, lemon zest and juice and olive oil.

Just before serving, mix the salmon with the lemon juice mixture and season. Taste for acidity and seasoning.

Pack into a ring mold and plate on a ring of cucumbers. Top with microgreens and lemon zest.

Serve immediately.

Serves 6-8

Better Than Sex

After the five o'clock platter of sandwiches, I decided there was little point in returning to my bunk. I brewed yet another shot of espresso and started preparing for the day. I began with the crew meal of *enchiladas*. I wrapped moist chicken and cilantro in corn tortillas, poured a chili laced tomato sauce over the wraps, and sprinkled crumbled *queso fresco* on top.

Chloe came into the galley at eight. Her dark hair was clipped back, revealing her clear green eyes. She looked perky and wide-awake. Her uniform was ironed and immaculate. I immediately felt self-conscious, knowing there were bags under my eyes and I still wore last night's crumpled polo.

Chloe handed me a coffee mug.

I took the mug and sipped. "Oww. That's hot."

"Sorry." Chloe smiled at me. "Did you get any sleep last night?"

"Not much. You?"

"A little." She smiled and shrugged. "How about after this charter is over we go for a day at the spa?"

I nodded. "A massage."

She smiled. "And a foot rub."

I laughed. "Maybe, I better start with a shower." I looked down at my uniform. "And a clean shirt."

* * * *

Later that day, while the guests were still asleep from their late night, I placed the enchiladas on the crew table, expecting everyone to dig in with vigor. I was slightly taken aback as I watched Gwen scrape off the topping and pick out the filling.

"Dairy allergy," she explained as she tucked a strand of blond hair behind her ear. "Sorry, it looks wonderful."

"No problem." I made a mental note to stock up on Almond milk and dairy-free cheeses. From that day forward, I would prepare a separate dish on the table with Gwen's name on a flag stuck in it. It would take little time and hardly any extra effort, but I would have to remember.

The next day, after another late night dinner, I had an extra hour in the morning with nothing to do while we waited for the guests to get up. I decided to bake a treat for the crew to welcome them to the new boat.

"What's that?" Gwen raised one eyebrow and stretched to peer over my shoulder as I placed a Tahitian vanilla cheesecake on the crew mess table. It was a fluffy full-of-dairy dessert.

"Sorry, this is cheesecake, but I have a soy version for you."

Gwen's smile disappeared. Her eyes drooped like a hound dog and her shoulders slumped forward. Her special plate held a grey-tinged stodgy round that sagged in the middle. It was a lifeless puddle next to the sheen of the cream cheese and sour cream version. One was bright and enticing, one was not. I had to admit, Gwen's soy cake was not the best substitution I'd come up with. I had pureed tofu and sugar with eggs and baked it. Even with my adventurous palate, I couldn't summon enough enthusiasm to try it.

"I have fresh raspberries to go with it." I tried to sound optimistic.

The rest of the crew wasted no time digging into the white creamy cheesecake. It was lighter than most baked cheesecakes and creamy moist. Dylan groaned in ecstasy as he took his first bite. "Heaven."

"Good shit," Stoyan added. He was Bulgarian and spoke six different languages. He would be a valuable interpreter in Greece and Italy, but English he had learned from watching porn movies and listening to rap music. Good shit was an eloquent compliment next to some of the other phrases he came out with.

"Thanks, Stoyan." I blushed.

I stole a sheepish glance at Gwen who was still staring at the tofu hockey puck. She seemed to be gathering the courage to lift her fork. Embarrassed, I left the room to avoid the look of disappointment on her face as she ate her dessert.

Anna was in the galley washing dishes when I entered.

"There's cheesecake downstairs," I told her.

"Oh, no thank you." She smiled sweetly. "I'm a vegan."

I tried to return her smile, but couldn't. "Really? Why didn't you say something?" I silently cursed Patrick's name for not asking about people's diets in their interview. Seafood allergy, dairy-intolerance, and now a vegan! I had enough to deal with without having to cater to ten different restrictions. From now on, I vowed, he would have to weed out picky eaters before they stepped onboard. *This isn't a restaurant,* I silently fumed.

"I didn't want to trouble you." Anna lowered her big brown doe eyes and looked at the floor, embarrassed to have even said something now.

My heart sunk. She was shy and up until now I'd been too busy with the new boat and guests to have a proper conversation with her. Suddenly, I felt I'd let her down. She was young, away from home for the first time, and living with a boatload of strangers. I should have made a greater effort to make sure she was okay. My anger at having to cook a special meal dissolved like an ice cube under hot water.

As the chef, I held a great deal of power for the happiness of the crew. I was the one responsible for their health, whether they ate healthy fresh foods or ones laden with pounds of butter, and whether they received food they like to eat. All crew come to a boat with likes, dislikes, and allergies to certain foods and, like it or not, it was my job to make sure everyone got fed.

With this new crew came a whole new set of recipe restrictions and requests I would have to figure out. Dylan was allergic to shellfish. A hint of seafood could send him into excruciating pain with knives stabbing through his stomach, so I would cook extra chicken or pork for him on the days I served shrimp or mussels. Gwen would get special meals when I used cheese or milk in a recipe, and now Anna would get grains and vegetables every meal. This would add an extra challenge to my day and help keep the offerings diverse.

"Don't ever worry about telling me something." I reached out and gave her a one-armed hug. "I'll be glad to cook vegan meals for you. It will give me something new to learn."

Fifteen minutes later, when tea break was over, I returned to the crew mess to clean up. I snuck another look at Gwen out of the corner of my eye. In front of her were two plates. One was licked clean. The other held the same grey blob I had left her with earlier.

I looked up astonished. She sat leaning against the couch, a smile played faintly on her lips. Her eyes rolled haphazardly. A dreamy, stupefied haze came over her face reminding me of pot-smoking stoners from high school.

"What are you doing?" I asked, not believing my eyes.

She looked at me with a guilty grin. "I couldn't help it."

"I thought you couldn't eat dairy?"

"I'll pay for this tonight."

"Then why?"

She looked at the limp, sweaty mold of soy in front of her then to the scraped clean plate. "It was worth it," she said. "This was better than sex."

Tahitian Vanilla Cheesecake

2/3 cup flour
3 tablespoons sugar
4 tablespoons butter

2 pounds cream cheese
1/2 cup sour cream
4 eggs
2 tablespoons Tahitian vanilla extract
1 cup sugar

1 cup sour cream
2 tablespoons sugar

Preheat the oven to 350 degrees. Place the flour, sugar, and butter in a food processor and grind until smooth. Spray a 12" spring form pan with non-stick spray. Press the crumble into the bottom and bake for 10 minutes until golden brown. Remove from oven and lower the temperature to 300 degrees. Wrap tinfoil around the bottom of the pan to create a "sleeve". This will block the waterbath seeping in and making the cheesecake soggy.

Place cream cheese, sour cream, eggs, vanilla and sugar in the food processor and puree until smooth. Pour over the crust. Cover with tinfoil. Place inside a large baking dish. Fill hot water into outer dish to come $\frac{3}{4}$ of the way up the spring form pan. Bake in oven for two hours until the center is no longer jiggly in the center.

~Continued on next page

Whisk together sour cream and sugar. Gently pour on top of hot cheesecake and return to oven, without the water bath for 10 minutes to set the topping.

Remove from oven and cool on counter for one hour. Wrap tightly in plastic wrap and refrigerate overnight to set.

Serve with tropical fruit sauces.

Makes one, 12-person cake.

Living the Dream

"C aptain," one of the Brazilian guests said to Patrick during the fourth day's six o'clock lunch. "Book me a helicopter for tonight." He paused. "Maybe we need two to fit us all."

Patrick's eyes went wide. He'd stopped by the table to check with them on their plans for the rest of the day. I was tableside de-boning a whole sea bass I had presented in a salt-crust. I listened, intrigued.

"Two helicopters?" Patrick repeated.

"Yes," the man replied as if he was talking to a child. "We have a table at Nikki Beach in St. Tropez tonight for dinner."

I didn't know whether to be astounded or relieved. *Who hired a helicopter to take them to dinner? Who cares?* This meant I had the night off.

* * * *

Patrick finally had time for a crew meeting. "So, I know this has been a crazy trip." There was laughter and a few vocal agreements from everyone sitting around the table. "But, we're half way through this week and everyone's doing a great job."

I nodded. He was the captain and leading the team, but I fully agreed.

"In thanks for all your efforts, everyone should go out and have a drink in town tonight." He smiled when a cheer went up from the table. "Victoria and I will stay onboard and wait for the guests to come back."

"Woo-hoo!" Nick, the mate, called out.

"But…" Patrick held up his hand. "Two drink max. We still have three more days left of this trip and guests onboard. Everyone has to be up and ready to work tomorrow."

He tried to look authoritative. The new crew may have been fooled, but I still remembered when he was the carefree, fun-loving crewmember who would not have stopped at two drinks. I smiled to myself, thinking how much had changed since he became captain.

The girls showered and changed as the boys hurried to turn on the deck lights and lower the flag. By ten, they had all left, and we were alone on the boat for the first time.

"Well captain," I said as I folded my arms around Patrick's neck. "What do you think of your new command?"

"Look at us." Patrick squeezed me tight. "We're living the dream." And with that he kissed me and the exhaustion and chaos of the week floated away.

I heard the crew door open and close three hours later. There were footsteps down the stairs, but by the time I reached the crew mess, Todd the deckhand was the only one there. He stood with the fridge door open, peering in. I had labeled the leftovers from dinner and placed them neatly on the top shelf. He grabbed the Tupperware marked *Bolognese* and shut the door.

"How was it?" I asked.

"Awesome." He scooped a heaping plate of noodles and sauce from a container. Dinner number two for him.

Hard-working boy. I thought, envious of his youth and fast metabolism.

"Everyone home?" I asked.

He nodded his head, his mouth full of pasta.

I left him to finish and went back to reading my magazine in the wheelhouse. Patrick's grandiose statement of "Victoria and I will cover" translated to little more than "Victoria will wait up until all hours of the morning for the guests while I fall asleep in my uniform on top of the bed." *It sure was nice to be the captain,* I thought.

I loved him, but I was tired too. My eyelids closed and my head fell forward, just to snap back at lightning speed and startle me awake. It was quiet on the boat with only the hum of the generator to keep me company. I lowered my eyelids again and this time jerked awake by almost falling off the stool I sat on. I looked at my watch. It was only twelve-thirty. I thought staying up to cook dinner all night was painful, but this might have been worse.

I watched the minutes tick by in a slow agonizing crawl around the clock. One o'clock, one-fifteen, one-thirty. I would never make it. Two o'clock took forever to arrive.

Finally, I heard a commotion on the aft deck. There was giggling and a man's louder laugh. The guests were home. I straightened my uniform and stole a quick glance at my hair to make sure I didn't look like I'd been sleeping on the job. I stuck my head in our cabin door.

"Patrick," I hissed.

He bolted straight up from his fetal position. "I'm up. I'm awake."

"Brush your teeth and come greet them."

Like a zombie, Patrick nodded and headed for the bathroom. I headed downstairs to start making drinks for them.

The laughter grew louder as I approached the deck. I came around the corner smiling, glad they were in a good mood. The smile froze on my face when I saw what they were laughing at.

There, on the deck, sprawled out, was our first mate, Nick. His chestnut brown hair spiked at ridiculous angles, his mouth hung open, drool slid down his face. His shirt was untucked, his pants undone and his shoes were kicked off in the corner. *Did he think he was in his cabin?*

I couldn't move. I didn't know what to do. The guests laughed even harder, jarring me out of my disbelief.

"Looks like he had a good night," one of them said.

"Better than ours," another chimed in.

"I… Uh…" I was speechless.

Just then, I heard Patrick's distinctive gait coming down the passageway. Like a slow-motion train wreck, I turned to try and block his view. I spun on my heel and started to speak. "Go back!" I wanted to yell. "You don't want to see this." But I couldn't. I just watched the scene before him play out on his face. Cheerfulness, recognition, shock, anger, and frustration washed over him. He too, just stood and stared.

The principal walked over and slapped him on the back, laughing. "Good luck with that one, Captain." He was still laughing as he led his party into the boat.

Patrick stayed glued to the spot. I didn't know what to do. *What do you say in a situation like this?*

Patrick knew. He stormed over to where Nick lay and grabbed him by the shoulder, shaking him awake. "Get up!" he seethed. "Do up your pants and get to bed."

Nick stumbled and slurred "Whaa…"

"Now!" I'd never heard Patrick like this. His voice was eerie calm. A shiver crawled down my back.

Nick slunk away. He ricocheted down the passageway and through the crew door.

Patrick's face was a mask betraying no emotion. "I'll go apologize to the guests." His voice was cold. "Make sure he gets to bed."

I nodded and turned to follow Nick, glad I wasn't the captain.

* * * *

The next morning, I was first one awake again. I left Patrick sleeping in the bunk. He had finally fallen asleep after spending hours staring at the ceiling, livid and boiling. I dared not say anything. There was nothing to say. This was bad. Nothing I said would make it any better. So, I lay beside him, wide-awake, staring at the same ceiling, wondering how he would handle things.

I turned on the lights and flipped the switch for the coffee machine, my morning ritual. I had gathered our laundry from the day before and descended the stairs to the crewmess to drop it in the hamper. When I turned to go back upstairs, I saw the note scrawled on the white board.

Have a nice summer, signed, *Nick.*

I laughed and rolled my eyes. *Drunk,* I thought and started up the stairs. But, then I got to thinking. *What did he mean?*

I hesitated and then turned around. I tiptoed down the crew corridor, trying not to wake anyone. I knocked softly on the port-forward door. "Nick?" I whispered.

There was no response.

"Nick?" I tried again. This time I twisted the handle of his door and slowly pushed it open. "Nick?"

It was dark in the room, but the shaft of light from the hall revealed a bed that had never been slept in. Drawers were open and empty, his bookshelf cleared of all personal belongings. I swallowed hard, but the lump in my throat would not go away. Nick had done a midnight runner.

I backed out of the room and stood in the hallway dazed. *What would I tell*

Patrick? Last night, he thought we were living the dream. This morning, it had turned into a nightmare.

Bolognese Sauce

1/4 cup butter
1/4 cup olive oil
4 cloves garlic, minced
1 onion, minced
1 celery stalk, minced
1 carrot, peeled and minced
1/2 teaspoon sea salt
18 grinds black pepper
2 pounds ground beef
1 pound ground pork
1/3 cup tomato paste
2 cups milk
2 cups red wine
1 - 28 oz can diced tomatoes
1 teaspoon sea salt
1/4 teaspoon nutmeg, grated
2 cups chicken stock
1 teaspoon sea salt
1 teaspoon sugar

Place butter and olive oil in a heavy-bottomed stockpot, over medium high heat. Sauté garlic, onions, celery, and carrot, stirring occasionally, until softened and golden about 10 minutes. Season with sea salt and pepper.

Add ground beef and pork and cook over medium high heat, stirring and breaking up lumps, until no longer pink, about 10 minutes.

Stir in tomato paste and cook 5 minutes. Pour in milk and simmer for 15 minutes until the liquid is almost evaporated. Pour in red wine and simmer for 15 minutes until the liquid is almost evaporated.

Add the diced tomatoes, sea salt, nutmeg, and chicken stock and gently simmer, covered, until sauce is thickened, 1 to 1 1/2 hours. Remove from the heat and skim the fat off the top. Stir in the last teaspoon of sea salt and sugar.

Taste for seasoning.

This sauce is best if left for a day in the fridge to meld the flavors.

Serves 8

Offerings

*T*he boat was quiet that day. So silent, you could hear the waves lapping against the hull. The story had spread through the crew faster than a bottle of peach schnapps at a high school dance. By ten everyone knew, but no one said a word to Patrick or me. Patrick had yet to descend the stairs from his office. Through the silence, I could hear him pacing and the odd slamming of the cabin door.

I had stood at the door gathering the courage to enter and even then, I began with a nervous smile. "Umm..."

After a minute of incoherent babble, Patrick became frustrated. "What is it, Victoria?" He sighed heavily. The early hour and lack of caffeine made him grouchy.

His gruffness shocked me into blurting out. "Nick left the boat."

Patrick roared to life like a Yamaha engine. He slammed his fist against the desk and swore loudly. "Are you kidding me?'

Like I could make this up. "No, he's gone."

Anger exploded out of him. He pushed past me and stormed into the pilothouse. He opened the cupboard where he kept everyone's passports and shuffled through the colors of each country. Nick's British burgundy one was missing. He must have come upstairs last night and grabbed it while we slept.

"Damn it!"

Those were the last words he said. He sequestered himself in the office. I dared not go up. The crew knew better than to disturb him. They avoided him and by extension me, all morning. There was the inevitable whispering and theories of what had happened, but no one came out and acknowledged the incident.

The guests were still asleep, so all I had to do was think and stew and worry about what would happen. I paced and ran scenarios through my head. *Would the guests be mad at the scene from last night? Would the manager think us incompetent to run a larger crew? Could we get through this?*

The buzz of the intercom startled me out of my spiraling thoughts.

"Victoria, will you send Dylan up here?" Patrick's voice was still spooky calm, giving no hint of what he was thinking. It scared me more than an outburst of rage.

"Sure." I said. "You okay?" Stupid question really.

"Just send him up." The intercom clicked off.

* * * *

Dylan was the bosun onboard. That meant he was the second deck position under Nick and ran the deck, while Nick was more of an overseer for the crew and a back-up for Patrick's role. They both held the same licensing, but Nick had more experience on bigger boats and had been offered the job originally. Apparently, licenses and experience didn't mean anything when you were shooting back Jack Daniels like buckets of water on a forest fire. By afternoon, the crew couldn't contain themselves, and one by one, started telling me the story from the night before. Gwen told me Nick arrived at the bar with the crew and proceeded to order and line up shots of Jack. In the hour and a half she was there he bought rounds not only for the crew, but for half the bar as well. When she left with Anna, he was already wobbling and slurring.

"He was trying to pick up the stew from the boat next door," she said. "So we all left him alone."

"Maybe that's why his pants were undone." Chloe laughed.

"I doubt it," Gwen replied. "He didn't seem to be getting very far."

"Hard to be impressive when you spill shots all over the girl," Todd said.

I rolled my eyes. "Classy."

Dylan came down from his meeting with Patrick. His broad handsome face was easy to read. His eyes lit with excitement.

"Well?" I asked.

His smile left no teeth uncovered. "You're looking at the new first mate."

"Congratulations!" I said, pleased with this easy solution. "And your position?" Even as the captain's wife, I knew little about what was going on until it had already happened.

Patrick came into the galley. "I just called Tom. He's finished his classes and can meet us in Italy next week."

"What about Katie?" I was confused. We didn't have a position available for her. Chloe, Gwen and Anna were all working out well.

"She's staying behind." Patrick shrugged. "Tom'll join us until September and then fly back to her."

I felt bad. I was glad Tom would be with us again, but a long-distance relationship was tough. As hard as it was for Katie to be on the boat, it would be worse for her to sit at home while Tom was off on one adventure after the next. Yachting tended to kill relationships. They rarely worked on board together twenty-four hours a day, and rarely worked on shore with one person sailing off and leaving the other behind. Patrick and I were lucky. So far we still liked each other.

* * * *

The day progressed without any more drama. Patrick calmed down and talked to the guests about the change in crew. He then made the necessary phone calls to inform the manager and the local authorities of Nick's midnight disappearing act. As captain, he was responsible for the crew. He brought us into different countries under his authority and had to handle the consequences of our actions. Customs officials in any country don't like to hear a captain has brought ten people into their country, but would be leaving with nine. Beyond the fact we were short a crewmember for work, Patrick could be in serious trouble for the stunt Nick pulled. Patrick could be escorted to a French jail that afternoon, or slapped with a substantial fine.

He was on the phone most of the afternoon explaining the situation, but didn't seem too agitated, so I assumed all would be well.

After crew dinner, I went into the interior to put away the serving platter I had used. I was crouched down behind the dining room table, reaching into the back of the cupboard when I heard voices in the hallway behind me.

"I hear congratulations are in order." It was one of the wives on the trip. Her thick South American accent was easy to recognize.

"Yes, thank you," Dylan replied politely.

I couldn't see them, but imagined them passing on the stairs. I stuck my head farther in the cupboard to rearrange the platters.

"I like a man in charge," the woman purred.

"Umm, well, I'm not actually in charge," Dylan stammered.

The conversation had my full attention now.

"My husband and friends are going out dancing again tonight," the woman said. "But I told them I have a headache." She paused. "Why don't you join me for a celebratory drink?"

"I, um, don't think…" Dylan stuttered.

"I like that too." Her voice was husky. "No thinking."

"I… I…"

"Meet me at one in the Jacuzzi."

I couldn't help it. I dropped the dish I was holding. Bang! The sound carried through the room and surely out to the hallway. I heard the woman laugh as she walked away.

Dylan came careening into the dining room, red-faced and breathing heavy. I'd been getting used to his seductive smile making the stewardesses blush, but this was way over the top.

I stood up and stopped him. "What was that?" I whispered.

Shaken and disbelieving he stuttered, "I … I don't know." He held out his hand for me to see. "She slipped me this."

In the palm of his hand he held a condom. The drama just ratcheted up a notch.

The French Market

*P*atrick listened to the story with more composure than I thought he would. He even cracked a smile at one point. To Dylan he said, "Don't worry. Just don't do anything!" To me, when we were alone in the bunk that night, he sighed heavily and just began giggling. I took that as a good sign.

"Remember the deckhand who ended up marrying the boss's daughter?" Patrick asked.

"How could I forget?"

The story was legend in the industry. One minute the kid was scrubbing the boss's teak deck and polishing his windows; four years later he was on his honeymoon aboard the yacht, sleeping in the master cabin.

"That could be Dylan." Patrick continued to laugh.

"Look at it this way," I said. "It can only get calmer from here."

He looked at me like I was crazy. "Are you kidding?" He took a deep breath. "This is only the beginning."

* * * *

The next morning, Patrick held his second crew meeting of the trip. After Dylan's encounter with the wife, we had to devise a strategy to keep her away from him.

"Todd, you're now on late duty with Gwen." Patrick didn't want Dylan to be caught alone again. Dylan didn't want to have anything to do with her, but he also couldn't insult her. This was tricky.

"Anna, you're to alert everyone in the morning when she wakes up."

"Afternoon, you mean," I corrected. None of the guests had shown their faces before two o'clock on this whole trip.

"Once she's awake, it's now everyone's job to chaperone." We were short-staffed already with Nick leaving, and now one of our able-bodied guys was a liability.

I looked at my watch. I needed to get going. The crew could figure out this schedule of babysitting without me. I raised my hand. "Can I be excused? I have to get to the market."

Patrick frowned but nodded his head. I jumped from the table and headed up the stairs as he ran down the plan for the day.

I walked out of the port and wandered past the ever-present red carpet of the film festival, over the dusty petanque courts, and down the promenade lined with cafes. The streets of Cannes were lined with Dijon-colored tall buildings decorated with narrow wrought-iron balconies, wooden shutters, and flower boxes. Above me, white shirts strung on a laundry line fluttered in the breeze. I passed my favorite little shop selling local cheeses and the *boulangerie* where the smell of warm baguettes floated out the door.

A feast of summer colors assaulted me as I entered the Forville Marche. Market tables sagged with tomatoes the color of fast cars. The shine of the eggplants' deep purple, almost black, skin formed a backdrop to the emerald green, slender zucchini. I searched for the freshest seasonal vegetables from tables laden with grey-green bulbs of baby artichokes still on the stalk, and mounds of wild mushrooms gathered from the nearby woods. The damp musk of the mushrooms lingered in the air. I picked up a long braid of garlic from the table in front of me, brought it under my nose, and breathed deeply. The heady smell invaded my senses.

"*S'il vous plait.*" I handed the garlic to the market woman.

I wandered to tables piled high with over twenty varieties of olives: black, wrinkled ones cured in sea salt sat beside pale green ones mixed with snipped herbs and whole cloves of garlic. Others floated in brine or were chopped to a fine paste to be used as a spread on baguettes. I popped a youthful, fat olive with smooth skin into my mouth as I'd selected more than I would use that day.

A line of little old ladies hunched over a table blocked my view of the fish selection. I wasn't sure what I would find. When I spotted the proprietor's fare and registered what it was, I couldn't help but corkscrew my face to one side. The veins in my neck bulged as I swallowed away the shock. On the table was a white plastic bucket, no different from one I mopped the galley floor with. The bucket itself wasn't the problem. It was what lay inside. The bucket was full of shiny, black eels slithering over and around each other like slimy snakes. I watched, transfixed. At the same moment, one of the eels lifted his head above the others and opened his mouth to breathe.

"I'll take two," I said, surprised at my own voice. I was traveling to experience new things, after all.

Next, I visited the woman who grew her own herbs. I couldn't escape the distinctive citric smell of lemon balm, the herbaceous smell of rosemary, and the lingering scent of fresh dill. This was the way to begin a day. Brightly colored vegetables accosted me at every turn.

"Victoria!" A woman behind me squealed. "*Ca va?*"

I turned and was wrapped in a hug by Martine, the voluptuous fruit seller. She stepped back and placed her dirt-stained hands on my shoulders, rounding herself in to kiss each cheek.

"*Cherie*, you are here again."

Every morning, this same woman filled my basket with a dozen, fist-sized white peaches from her garden. Each day I had devoured more than my share, standing over the galley sink, juice dribbling down my chin. I gobbled the subtle flesh as sweetness swirled through my mouth. I would finish one and reach for another. By the end of the day, they had all disappeared. The next morning, I would return to Martine to start the cycle again.

"Bonjour." I stammered. She giggled and picked up a peach.

"For you, *cherie*."

I smiled and headed back to the boat, planning the days menu from the vegetables in the cloth bag that hung over my shoulder, while enjoying peach after peach.

I wiped my sticky hands on my skort as I entered the marina.

As I hurried down the quai, past dozens of other shiny white yachts, I got a funny feeling in my stomach. I walked past six more yachts and turned back around. I peered down the row of aft decks and spun back to look the other way. Guests sat on the back of a few of the boats having breakfast and sipping coffee, but no one I knew. I retraced my steps again, paying more attention to each boat. There was a Lazzara and a Feadship, a Lurrsen and Warren but none I recognized. I began to panic. Our boat was gone.

I walked the quai one more time, but I was sure of the slip the boat had been in. It was now empty.

A flood of worry washed over me. I needed to be on board getting breakfast ready. *What if the guests woke up and I wasn't there?* I chewed on the side of my thumb while a sudden realization hit me. *Patrick had left without me!*

Gutsy

*I*t didn't take me long to figure out what to do. I stood on the dock, in front of our empty slip, under the blazing hot sun, and flipped my cell phone open. My heart raced. I was torn between being furious with Patrick and panicked. I needed to be onboard preparing for the flurry of food these guests requested. I didn't have time for this.

"Hello, Patrick speaking." His voice was calm and professional.

I waited a beat.

"Hello?" he said again.

"Did you forget something?" My voice dripped with sarcasm.

"Like what?" Patrick's voice was light and sing-songy.

"Like me!" I couldn't believe he would do this. *Me of all people!*

"Where are you?" Again, all nursery rhyme-like.

"Patrick!" My voice was panic and frustration. "I'm on the dock! I was at the market! You left! I have to make breakfast!" The deckhand on the boat next to the empty slip looked over at the crazy lady screaming into her cellphone. "Get back here and get me!"

There was silence on the other end.

"Patrick!"

I could hear soft giggling over the line. "Victoria, look to your left."

I whipped my head around frantically to see Dylan sitting in our inflatable at the tender dock. He waved. I sighed and felt all the tension and strain from lack of sleep fall away. My heart surged. He didn't forget. I, too, began to giggle. I should have known he was a better captain and husband than that.

"The guests requested we move to the Ile Saint-Marguerite for the morning. We'll meet you and Dylan there." Patrick was still laughing.

"You better." I tried to sound mad, but couldn't. "Doesn't look good, leaving your wife behind."

Patrick's voice changed to one of heartfelt seriousness. "I would never do that."

* * * *

And, like every trip, the end came, whether we believed it ever would or not. The requisite bottles of champagne flowed to celebrate the completion and we all laughed at everything that happened.

"That was some beginning," Chloe said as she filled her glass a second time.

"One I would rather not repeat." Patrick held his glass out for more.

All agreed. The crew made plans to go out for the evening, their wallets bulging with Euros from the tip. This time there were no drink limit and no repercussions for stumbling back to the boat drunk. It was almost expected.

But not for me. I'm not sure when it happened, but I was either too old, or had too many other things to do to join in on the celebration. Patrick and I stayed aboard to watch the boat while everyone one else went to explore the Cannes nightlife.

"Have I told you how much I love this new boat?" Patrick asked for the hundredth time since we came onboard.

"You can say it again." I wound my arms around his neck and kissed him.

He looked me in the eye like we were renewing our vows. "I love our life."

I kissed him again. I couldn't agree more.

* * * *

"I'll pick up the guests at one-thirty," Patrick said. We were in our pre-charter meeting. A week and a half had passed since the all-nighters left. Everyone had caught up on sleep and was ready to go again. We moved the boat from Cannes to Naples to pick up the next set of guests. "There will be six of them."

I started planning their lunch in my head as he ran down the list of names and pertinent details. I wasn't listening. I had the information I needed.

I had no preference sheet for these guests, but that was okay. We would be cruising the island of Capri and the Amalfi coast all the way to Sardinia. Anything we needed, I could send someone ashore to pick up. I would make their first meal a buffet with plenty of options and then quiz them afterward to plan the rest of the trip.

The next morning, I printed the menu:

Welcome to Italy

Insalata Caprese
Panzanella
Cacciucco
Pizza Margherita
Vitello Tonnato

I felt confident this gave them a wide range of flavors and ingredients to choose from.

Like always, as the time approached, we lined up on the aft deck. I smiled at Tom, glad he was back with us. He'd flown in four days earlier and had instantly fit in with this new crew. He was fresh from his first set of classes and just as eager to prove himself as he was on his first day of the last boat. I smiled, thinking how different this boat would be for him.

My smile faded the moment the first man stepped on board. I knew I had a problem. As if his shiny designer loafers and tailored white shirt weren't enough of a give away, his dark curls and olive complexion sent terror through me. My heart began to pound as I watched a slim, well-dressed woman board after him. One-by-one my fear built with the addition of each guest.

An older man wearing a fedora spoke first. He reached for the *bellini* that Chloe offered and said, "*Bellisimo!*"

Every last shred of hope vanished in that moment. The guests were Italian.

"I don't understand what the problem is?" Chloe asked while we put lunch out. "They seemed nice."

"The problem isn't with them. It's me," I said. "I made Italian food for Italians."

Chloe looked at me and laughed. "Gutsy."

I started slicing the veal. *Was it thin enough? Did the sauce have enough lemon?* This was a recipe I had made dozens of times, always to rave reviews, but never to people who had eaten their mom's version since birth. *How would mine stand up? How dare I even try?*

"It'll be fine," Chloe said as she carried the cutlery out to set the table.

Just as I was stirring the last of the seafood into the stew, the older man wearing a silk suit entered the galley. He was a big man with meaty hands and folded jowls.

"Ah, it smells wonderful in here." He wandered over to the stove and peered in my pot. Small bubbles exploded on the surface of the liquid. Wisps of the sea floated into the air and mingled with the smell of garlic. "It reminds me of my kitchen."

I relaxed a little. "At home?"

"No, I don't cook much at home." He cupped his hand and waved it over the rising steam, directing it toward his face and breathed deeply. "Just in the restaurant."

My spirit fell like a deflated *soufflé*. Not only was this man Italian, but he was a chef as well. Could there be any more pressure on this lunch?

To say I was nervous was an understatement. My hand shook as I plated an arugula salad and cut the *focaccia* into squares. *What was I thinking?*

"It looks fabulous," Chloe said as she carried the platters out to the sky deck.

I fidgeted and fluffed around the galley, waiting for the report. She returned a few minutes later, smiling, but it looked like it was more out of pity.

"Go ahead, tell me." I clenched my jaw, ready for the report.

"They're enjoying it, only…" she paused, searching for the right words or the courage to tell me.

"Yes?" My stomach twisted like a dishtowel being rung out.

"I heard them talking." She paused again. "The man's not only a chef, but owns a Michelin-starred restaurant."

I groaned loudly and grasped the counter in front of me. My knees wobbled. "Are you kidding me?"

Michelin is the top standard in the food world. A star is practically impossible to get without being a master chef and at the top of your game.

Chloe shook her head. "No, but they're smiling and laughing."

"Yeah, at me!"

The more time passed, the more nervous I became. I felt like throwing up. I was serving them the most basic of recipes. Being a Michelin-starred chef, he was used to an elevated cuisine; one of multiple flavors, textures and techniques. I panicked and immediately decided on an Asian-themed dinner and Mexican for lunch the next day. I wouldn't make the same mistake twice. It was bad enough cooking for a chef, but serving dishes he'd perfected over years of training and testing was just ludicrous.

Chloe returned with the empty plates. "They want to speak with you."

I blanched and stalled for time. I searched for words of apologies. I removed my apron, folded it meticulously, and left it on the counter.

I rounded the corner to see the chef place his fork down on his plate. He looked up as I approached the table. "Victoria, where did you learn this recipe?" He gestured to the platter of meat.

I swallowed. "From the butcher where I bought the veal."

He nodded and picked up his fork again. "Did you taste it?"

Oh no, oh no, oh no. I gulped. "Yes." I sounded like a mouse.

"Then you know," he began. He lifted another slice of veal to his plate. He cut it slowly and skewered the piece on the tines of his fork and raised it for me to see. He studied it a moment and then popped it into his mouth. His face broke into a smile. "This is exactly how it should taste!" He stood up and raised his glass of Chianti. "*Bellisimo, bella.*"

The others nodded and smiled. I felt my knees go weak.

"For cooking like that, we want to name you an honorary Italian citizen."

He may just have been being gracious, but I couldn't help but smile and wish it were true.

Vitello Tonnato

Poaching Liquid:
10 cups chicken stock
1 cup white wine
1 onion
2 carrots
2 stalks celery
5 whole cloves garlic
2 stalks rosemary
1 teaspoon black peppercorns
1 teaspoon sea salt
4 bay leaves

1 veal tenderloin

~Continued on next page

Sauce:
1 cup mayonnaise (see page 82 for recipe)
1/2 cup olive oil
1 cup canned tuna in oil, drained
3 anchovies
2 tablespoons lemon juice
3 tablespoons capers

Garnish:
Capers
Parsley
Lemon slices

One day before serving:
    Bring chicken stock, wine, onion, carrots, celery, garlic, rosemary, black peppercorns, sea salt and bay leaves to a boil in a heavy bottomed pan. Simmer for 15 minutes. Add veal tenderloin and reduce heat to medium-low. Simmer for 20 minutes, until center of tenderloin registers 110 degrees on a meat thermometer. Cool tenderloin in the liquid overnight.
    Puree mayonnaise, olive oil, tuna, anchovies, lemon juice and capers in a food processor until smooth. Refrigerate over night.

Next day:
    Remove veal from liquid and slice thinly. Spiral on a platter, on top of arugula creating a thin base. Spread the top with sauce.
    Garnish with chopped capers, parsley and lemon slices

Serves 6

Margherita Pizza

Dough:
1 envelop dry yeast
2 cups warm water
1 teaspoon sugar
1/2 cup whole-wheat flour
4-1/4 cups all-purpose flour
1 teaspoon sea salt
2 tablespoons olive oil

~Continued on next page

Toppings:
Non-stick spray
1/4 cup semolina flour
2 cups tomato sauce
6 balls fresh mozzarella, sliced $\frac{1}{4}$ inch thick
1-1/2 cups shredded fresh basil
1 teaspoon sea salt

Making the dough:

In the bowl of a stand mixer, mix together yeast, $\frac{1}{4}$ cup warm water and sugar. Let stand until mixture creates a bubbling foam, approximately 5 minutes. On medium low speed, mix together the rest of the warm water, whole-wheat flour, all-purpose flour, sea salt and olive oil. Mix on medium speed for 5 minutes until dough is smooth, soft and elastic. The amount of flour may vary depending on moisture content of your flour. The dough should pull away from the bowl while kneading. If your bowl is clean after mixing you have the right consistency. If not, add more flour until desired consistency is reached.

Cover the bowl with plastic wrap and let rise in a warm place for one hour until it has doubled in bulk.

Creating the pizza:
Preheat oven to 400 degrees.

Divide dough into six equal portions. On a floured surface roll one dough portion into a thin round crust. Transfer to a baking sheet that has been sprayed with non-stick spray and dusted with semolina flour to prevent sticking.

Prick the crust with a fork to avoid bubbles. Coat the top of the crust with tomato sauce, making sure not to apply too thick. Arrange slices of mozzarella over the sauce allowing space for it to spread as it melts. Season with sea salt.

Repeat with remaining pizzas.

Bake for 20 minutes, rotating trays half way through to obtain even cooking. When the crust is golden brown and the cheese is melted and bubbling remove from oven. Sprinkle top with shredded basil. Slice in six and serve.

Makes 6 medium pizzas

Secrets

We were keeping a dangerous secret. It might not destroy lives or lead to catastrophe, but I was pretty sure it would be embarrassing if we were caught. Too late to think about that now, because dinner was half over and we were all in this together.

Everything started early that morning when I was preparing to go to the market. Once again, I was in the crew mess earlier than anyone else. While checking how many lettuces were in the fridge, I heard a cabin door squeak shut. Involuntarily, I glanced down the dark hallway to see Tom tiptoeing away from the cabin Chloe shared with Gwen. He didn't see me. Just as quietly, he opened his cabin door and slipped inside.

I looked at my watch. It was five in the morning. That could only mean one thing. It didn't shock me. Crew hooked up all the time. That was only natural. But, Tom had only joined us a month before. And, as far as I knew, Katie was waiting for him back home to finish the summer charter season and return to her. I felt sad. I'd hoped they could work it out.

I finished stocktaking and set off for the market, leaving a note for Patrick that I was off the boat. Under the cloak of darkness, through an ancient stone passageway, I met with the other chefs of the yachts in the marina. The four of us had stumbled, tired and groggy to the market each morning in search of inspiration. This was the third morning we'd all convened at the same time.

"Morning," I mumbled to Pete, the Australian chef from next door. "How was the quail last night?" I'd watched him haggle with the vendor over price the day before.

"Awesome." He had more energy than I that morning. My mind was still troubled by what I'd witnessed in the crew hallway. "I marinated it in rosemary and lemon."

We stood talking recipes while Tara from two boats down joined us. "Is the fish guy here yet?"

I nodded in the direction of the alley, where a white van had just arrived. A squat man in white rubber boots and apron opened the back doors. Chips of ice spilled onto the cobblestones. The fishing fleet was docked in the marina down the road. Each morning, the same man drove the mile and a half to the market to sell the fleet's catch. We all crowded around the back of the van.

"*Ciao.*" His face was lined with the life he led. "Today the sea was good."

He waved his rough, thick-fingered hand over the display of seafood in front of him. It felt a little like we were trading on the black market. The snow-white flesh of monkfish glistened beside a Styrofoam box of the spiked shells of cockles and another box of coral-crusted langoustines. In other boxes, the probing necks of razor clams protruded from their elongated shells while slow-moving lobsters crawled over each other.

"I like the look of those prawns." Richard pointed to the pile of plump pink crustaceans. He had just arrived and was peering over my shoulder. "Maybe as a salad appetizer?"

I nodded in agreement.

"There are those cannellini beans in the fresh market," Tara added. "Maybe as a puree underneath?"

"Salmon for tartar?" Pete ventured.

"That's what I made last night," Rick countered.

"Tuna?" The fishmonger gestured at the deep rose loin of a yellowfin on ice.

"Seared with wasabi and bok choy," Pete agreed.

I listened intently to the other chefs. I always liked bouncing ideas off other people and missed the camaraderie that came from working in a kitchen with other chefs, but so far nothing had jumped out at me. Maybe I was just having an off day. I liked the idea of the prawns, but wasn't keen on the tuna.

It was strange. We still had the Italian chef and his friends on board. I tried serving other cuisines, but they had requested local fare. I agreed what we could find in the markets here in Sicily was better suited for Italian menus, but I was still nervous about my interpretation of the dishes. This had been a long three-week charter. The work wasn't harder work than normal; in fact, with only six guests it was relatively easy, but I fretted over each and every meal like I was serving royalty. They had been gracious and said they liked everything, but that night was the last dinner, and I wanted to make sure it was just right. I was listening to the other chefs, but I had to put together the perfect combination and was leaning in a different direction.

"How about the monkfish?" I pointed to the lustrous white flesh on ice. "With *caponata* vegetables?"

The fishmonger bowed his head. His dark wavy hair fell to his eyes. "Ah, you know the food of Sicily."

I held up my thumb and forefinger half an inch apart. "*Piccolo.*"

His guttural laugh reverberated down the alley. "Ah, bella, you are right. The monkfish is very good today." He made an okay sign with his work-worn right hand. "It is good with the *caponata.*"

I blushed, embarrassed by the attention. The rest of the chefs nodded and agreed to the choice.

"It is decided then." The fishmonger spoke English like he was reciting from a textbook. He pointed to Pete and Richard, who both nodded their heads.

"Two kilos of the prawns and three kilos monkfish," Tara said.

The fishmonger's hand plunged into the pile. Long wisps of the prawn's antennae trailed through his fingers. He weighed them, studied the scale, and plucked two more from the pile before thrusting them into a plastic bag. Next, he scooped up the white fillet and placed it in the sculpted groove of the thick wooden cutting board worn from use. Years of butchering fish for people in the seaport and visiting yachts meant this man could produce three kilos without measuring. He ran his curved saber-like knife through the flesh and smiled when the scales confirmed his estimation. As he bagged the fish, he raised his bushy eyebrows to me.

"I'll take three of each," I said.

As he handed me my bag, I kissed the fishmonger on each cheek, "*Grazie tanto!*"

He cupped my face in his hands. The smell of the sea surrounded me. "Ah, *bella. Domani?*"

"Yes, I'll be back tomorrow." I said my goodbyes to the other chefs and headed for the vegetable stand, knowing I would return again the next morning at first light to repeat the ritual.

I didn't see the other chefs all day. Richard's boat left the dock to anchor for fun in the azure waters. The tender to Tara's boat zoomed away a few hours later, laden with coolers and umbrellas for the beach. But, by seven o'clock each boat had squeezed back on the dock, lined up like fingers pressed together in a salute. As the sun sank away to brighten someone else's day, the tables on each aft deck were set with fine china and crystal glasses. Chloe and Gwen were busy polishing silverware and Todd turned on the deck lights.

Chloe returned to pick up the water glasses. I decided to ask. "So, you and Tom?" She'd worked on enough boats to know there were never any secrets.

She laughed and brushed the hair out of her eyes. "Not me," she said, leaving the rest of the story obvious.

Gwen came in to grab the window cleaner. Being Scandinavian, she was tall and blond, completely opposite Katie. Maybe that was the attraction. Something new. I opened my mouth to say something, but thought better of it. I no longer worked with Katie, but I had to finish the season with Gwen. I didn't want her to feel awkward or embarrassed around me.

I kept what I saw to myself and began peeling the prawns. This was a mindless job and as my fingers worked through the pile, I started to fret about the other secret I was keeping. *Would the guests laugh if they found out? Would the chef be mad or would he appreciate the situation?* I'd already printed the menu. There was no going back now.

Later that evening, as I pooled the vegetables on the gold-rimmed plate in front of me, I bit my lip. This all could go horribly wrong.

As Chloe left with the last meal, I stuck my head out of the galley and looked for my co-conspirators. Sandwiched beside our boat were three other gleaming white floating palaces. All aft decks had elegant tables set with different colors and themes. All tables had glamorous guests dressed in the latest fashion. All guests had perfectly styled pretty food in front of them. And each plate held exactly same thing.

Instead of each yacht having their own personal chef, we had collaborated and served the same meal to every single guest on the dock that night.

Seared Shrimp
with White Bean Puree and Proscuitto

1 (16 ounce) can cannelini beans, rinsed and drained
1 lemon, juiced
2 tablespoons olive oil
1/4 cup chicken stock
4 sprigs thyme, destemmed and chopped
1/2 teaspoon sea salt
12 grinds black pepper

1/2 cup olive oil
8 cloves garlic, chopped
2 pounds shrimp, peeled and deveined
1 teaspoon sea salt
18 grinds black pepper

6 slices prosciutto, chopped into "bacon bits"
4 cups arugula
2 tablespoons olive oil
1/2 lemon, juiced
1/4 teaspoon sea salt

In a food processor, puree the cannellini beans, lemon juice, olive oil, chicken stock, thyme, sea salt and pepper. Warm in a small pot over medium-low heat.

Heat a heavy bottomed sauté pan on high. Add 2 tablespoons olive oil and 2 cloves of garlic. Add $\frac{1}{4}$ of the shrimp and season with some of the sea salt and pepper. Sauté 2 minutes on each side until they are just cooked through. The flesh will turn from opaque to white. Be careful not to overcook them or they will turn tough and chewy. Scrape the pan into a bowl with a rubber spatula and repeat process working in batches for the rest of the shrimp.

Return the pan to the heat and sauté the prosciutto until crisp.

Divide puree amongst 6 salad plates as a pool in the center of the plate. Place the shrimp around the outside of the puree.

Toss the arugula in olive oil and lemon juice. Season with sea salt. Use your hand to bunch a "ball" of arugula to place on top of the puree. Sprinkle the crispy prosciutto on top.

Serves 6

Monkfish with Caponata

Caponata
1 eggplant, diced to 1" cubes
2 teaspoons sea salt
6 celery stalks, diced to 1/4" pieces
1/4 cup olive oil
4 cloves garlic, minced
1 red onion, diced to 1/4" pieces
1 red peppers, diced to 1/4" pieces
1/2 teaspoon sea salt
1 - 16 ounce can diced tomatoes
1/2 cup kalamata olives, chopped
1/2 cup green olives, chopped
3 tablespoons capers
16 grinds black pepper
1/4 cup olive oil
4 cloves garlic, minced
3 tablespoons pine nuts

1/3 cup red wine vinegar
2 tablespoons sugar
3 tablespoons parsley, chopped

Mix sea salt and diced eggplant and place in a colander to drain for 1 hour. This removes the eggplants bitter bite.

Blanch celery in salted water for 1 minute. Drain and set aside.

In a heavy-bottomed skillet, over medium-high heat, sauté garlic and onions in olive oil for 3 minutes until soft. Add red peppers and sauté for another 3 minutes. Add tomatoes, olives, and capers. Reduce heat to medium-low. Cover and simmer for 10 minutes. Add black pepper and remove from heat.

Rinse the eggplant to remove bitter juices and salt and pat dry with paper towels. In a heavy-bottomed skillet, heat olive oil over medium-high heat. Sauté eggplant and garlic for 8 minutes to soften. Stir in celery.

Add the eggplant to the tomato mixture and return the empty skillet to the heat. Toast the pine nuts by stirring for 3 minutes over medium-high in the dry pan until they turn golden. Remove to the tomato mixture. Add vinegar and sugar to pan and reduce by half. Mix all together with parsley.

Check seasoning and serve warm or at room temperature.

~Continued on next page

The Monkfish:
2 tablespoons olive oil
6 six-ounce monkfish loins
1 teaspoon sea salt
12 grinds black pepper
1/4 cup flour

Preheat oven to 350 degrees.
Heat the olive oil in a heavy-bottomed skillet over high heat. Season the monkfish with sea salt and pepper and dust with flour. Add the monkfish to the pan and cook until golden-brown. Transfer fish to a cookie sheet and roast in the oven for 15 minutes.
Serve each monkfish loin on a bed of warm caponata.

Serves 6

A Day Off

The days ceased to have names and melded into one another. We were on our third set of guests of the summer with only a few days between each trip. The chef and his friends had departed and two day later four couples from Greece and Turkey arrived. I was weary. The crew was exhausted.

"Victoria, we'll skip lunch today and just have an assortment of local delicacies. A buffet spread for us to graze from," the latest of our guests announced. This was the longest charter we had done so far. They had already been onboard for two weeks and we were exploring the Greek islands for the next two. I looked over my shoulder to the tuna loin I'd been marinating and the salads already prepared. I'd been up since five baking bread and creating a dessert for lunch. I sighed, knowing there wasn't anything I could do to sway the lunch back to what I'd already prepared. The woman was oblivious to the food around her. "It's ten-thirty now—let's say at two o'clock?"

We were three miles from Athens and the only local delicacies I had onboard were from our last country—Italy.

"How soon until we're docked?" I asked Patrick.

He looked at the GPS. "Twenty minutes."

I looked at my watch and bit my lip. "That long?"

"Probably longer. It'll take us awhile to maneuver into the slip."

I picked up my cell and called to arrange a taxi to the fresh market. By the time Tom and Dylan had thrown the first line, a black car waited for me. I jumped to shore, cloth bags in hand, before the boys even had the passerelle assembled. It was now six minutes after eleven, and I had provisions to obtain.

George, an olive-skinned man with three days stubble held open the car door for me. "I take you to the market." He flashed a thousand-watt smile that revealed perfectly straight white teeth, then pushed dark glasses that held his shoulder-length curls off his face to his eyes. I had my own private chariot from Mount Olympus. "Do you know Greek cuisine?" he asked.

I hadn't been to Greece before. We had picked the guests up in Italy and sailed through the islands of Croatia and up the fjords into the ports of Montenegro. In Greece, we docked in Corfu for a night, but left early the next morning to pass through the Corinth Canal, so I had little time to step off the boat. I knew I could make Greek salad, *mousakka* and *souvlaki* from recipes I'd gathered at home, but I guessed my versions were far from what locals ate.

"No, and I'd love some guidance." I looked at my watch again, eleven-fifteen. "I'm in a bit of a rush."

George flashed his Adonis smile again. "I take you for true Greek fare." His broken English and heavy accent added to his allure.

The streets of Athens careened past us in a blur. He climbed away from the marina along the ocean road, taking corners like a Formula One driver. My leg jostled up and down, not only from the bumps in the road, but with impatience. I was cutting it close to gather groceries and get back on board in time for a two o'clock lunch. *Why didn't I just tell the woman I couldn't do it?* Because, in this industry, you rarely said no.

George pulled into the market and directed me toward the first vendor. Purple-black almond-shaped olives lay piled in bins. Water bottle plastic jugs of thick green olive oil lined the back of the stall.

"First you need kalamata olives and oil for the taste of Greece," George tutored. "This and a little lemon juice on everything." George mimicked squeezing a lemon and grabbed two bottles of oil as a wrinkled woman in a black polyester dress weighed a kilogram of olives for us. We raced around the corner to the next stall.

At eleven-forty, we skidded to a stop in front of a table of local fish, squid and octopus displayed on palates of ice. "I'll take two octopus." I pointed at the mauve-tinged tentacles tangled on the ice.

"The best is to catch the octopus in the rocks by shore," George told me. "Leave it to dry on the beach while you swim." Again in mime, he breast-stroked his way forward. "Take it home. Boil it in wine with some onions and carrots for two hours." He held up two fingers to make sure I understood. "This is my favorite way." George tapped his chest, proud to be dispelling such precious knowledge.

I looked at my watch.

"I don't have two hours."

George spoke loud and animated in Greek to the man behind the counter. The fishmonger put the octopus I had pointed out back on the ice and reached for another in a bin behind him.

"This one is already cooked." George said. "Maybe today you just grill it with some oregano, olive oil and lemon juice."

At ten to twelve, George slapped the palm of his hand to his forehead. "Ah, Florina peppers." He grabbed my hand and pulled me toward the pile of red capsicums. "These you fry and serve with sea salt." George handed eight fire-engine red long peppers to the vegetable lady to weigh. "Maybe when you have time, you roast them to get a deep sweet flavor." He swung his head to the display of eggplants to his left. "And these aubergines. They're sweeter, not so bitter. Good for salad." George handed four snow-white bulbs to the same woman.

"Thank you," I called to the woman over my shoulder as George directed me back toward the car.

"You need pies," he said. "Lots of spinach, some leek, and maybe a cheese."

Individual filo parcels wrapped in triangle, cigar and square shapes went into a paper bag. Again, I looked at my watch. Twelve-fifteen.

"That should be good," I said. "Thank…" George wasn't listening. He pulled me into a storefront outside the market.

"Quick, we need baklava and sesame bread." This had become a challenge for George. He seemed determined not to let me down.

The last stop was for feta cheese, *haloumi* and thick tangy yogurt at a makeshift stand on the corner. It looked rickety, like the lemonade stands I used to construct as a kid. But George assured me this was the best in the area.

"Mix this with a grated cucumber and garlic." He thrust a plastic container of yogurt in the cloth bag and turned back for one last thing. "Maybe with these *dolmades*." He indicated to add two-dozen vine-leaf-wrapped parcels to our bag.

By twelve-thirty we were back in his cab and driving at the speed of light.

George swiveled in his seat to continue my Greek cooking lesson. "Use half the yogurt for dip and spoon the rest into a dish with honey and chopped walnuts." Traffic whizzed past us. "Fry the peppers first in a hot pan, and last the cheese, just quick. Squeeze lemon over it." Again, he mimicked the squeezing of citrus.

"And Greek salad?" I asked.

"Bah," George sputtered. "All salads are Greek—you are in Greece!"

I laughed. He was right. *Silly tourist.*

"But there are tomatoes and cucumbers in the bag." He'd been so fast I hadn't even seen him buy them. George could be a yacht chef. He was good at this game.

We pulled up to the back of the boat, and I jumped from the back seat.

"Don't put the *baklava* in the fridge." George doled out his last pieces of advice. "Serve it with the figs and the yogurt." He kissed me on both cheeks. "Good luck," he said before speeding off like I was still in a hurry and in the car. Maybe that was just George's normal state of movement.

In the galley, I emptied my bags on the counter and began assembling our local feast. I fried the peppers and grilled the octopus. Numerous times I repeated his action of squeezing the lemon. It went into and on top of everything with a generous splash of olive oil.

With two minutes to spare, I took the last of the *haloumi* out of the searing hot pan and plated the spinach pies. Chloe, Gwen and I carried the dishes to the table at precisely two o'clock.

Chloe announced lunch was served and the guests crowded round as I placed the eggplant salad on the table. The woman who had originally spoken to me about the lunch looked pleased.

"Just some local foods to nibble on," she said. "I gave Victoria the day off."

Thinking of the race around the market, the untouched lunch I'd been preparing, since the wee hours of the morning and the scramble to plate everything. I smiled and headed back to the galley to clean up and start dinner for the crew. I loved being at the market with George. This was a good day off.

Dolmades

1 jar of preserved grape leaves
1/2 cup olive oil
2 cloves garlic, minced
2 cups onions, finely chopped
1 cup basmati rice
1-1/2 cups water
1 teaspoon sea salt
24 grinds black pepper

1/4 cup pine nuts
1/4 cup dried currants

Greek yogurt
Lemon wedges

Boil 1 gallon water.
Remove leaves from jar and unroll. Drop them into boiling water and remove from heat. Let them to soak for 5 minutes. Drain and cool.

The filling:
Heat $\frac{1}{4}$ cup olive oil in heavy 12-inch skillet over moderate heat. Add onions and garlic and stir for 5 minutes until soft. Add rice and stir constantly for 2 minutes. Add water, sea salt, and pepper. Bring to a boil over high heat. Reduce heat, cover, and cook 15 minutes until rice is cooked and liquid is absorbed. Remove rice to a large bowl and return the skillet to medium heat.
Brown the pine nuts in the skillet for 5 minutes, shaking pan occasionally, until golden. Add pine nuts and currants to rice.

Stuffing and rolling the dolmades:
Place a leaf in front of you, dull-side up and snip off the stem. Spoon a tablespoon of filling just above the place where you cut off the stem, leaving room on both sides. Fold the two flaps up over the filling. Fold in the sides. Roll the wrapped filling from bottom to top of leaf like a cigar. Place roll in a large, heavy bottomed sauté pan, seam side down. Repeat until there is no more stuffing. Stack rolls side by side as tightly as possible.

Cooking:
Sprinkle dolmades with two tablespoons of oil and pour in 1 cup of cold water. Place sauté pan on high heat until water is boiling. Then reduce heat to low and simmer, tightly covered, for 40 minutes. You may need to add another cup of water after twenty minutes.
Uncover and cool.
Serve with lemon wedge and Greek yogurt for dipping.

Makes 40

International Incident

*I*t was just a simple lunch. How was I supposed to know I'd start a war?

Three days later, we were anchored in a secluded bay off of Crete on the edge of the Aegean Sea for our guests to enjoy the last of the summer's warm water and fading light. That afternoon they gathered around the table, embracing and kissing each other on each cheek as if they hadn't just spent the last twenty days together doing the exact same thing. Chloe poured shots of ouzo they skulled in seconds. They leapt to their feet and commenced another round of affection while Chloe refilled the glasses. They were a passionate group.

I set a platter of grilled lamb skewers on the table.

"Ah, *sis kebap*," the Turkish woman raised her glass in a toast.

"Bah, this is Greek food." Nico, the man with wild bushy eyebrows spat before tipping back another shot. "*Souvlaki!*"

"No, no. This is Turkish dish." She dismissed him.

Nico grabbed a skewer and waved it in front of her. "Greek!" He stated with utter certainty.

Both of them glared at each other and then turned and looked at me for confirmation. I thought for a moment how to be diplomatic. After the Italian food for an Italian chef, I'd been hesitant to attempt ethnic dishes of the guests' home country. But here we were in Greek waters, bordering Turkey, and they requested local dishes. I'd called on George more than once to walk me through a meal.

"It's lamb marinated in olive oil, garlic, and spices." To me it was a skewer, I didn't want to label it to a particular region.

"Ha! See, like I said. It is Greek." Nico puffed out his chest, folded his arms, and smiled.

"Tsk." The woman squeezed the sound between her clenched teeth. "She is serving it with *cacik*." She pointed to the bowl of yogurt and grated cucumbers Gwen had placed in the center of the table next to soft flat bread and herb salad.

"That's not *cacik*." Nico's voice rose in pitch. "Everyone knows this is *tzatsiki*." He picked up the spoon and held it a foot above the dish, letting the sauce dribble down like a leaky faucet to show his companions.

Once again, all eyes shifted to me. *Why was I the mediator?* Nico was right, the recipe I used for the yogurt dish was from a Greek cookbook, but the lamb marinade was a Turkish recipe. I started to panic. *Could I mix the cultures like that?*

I was saved from answering when the Turkish woman's husband spoke. "It is undeniably Turkish. We ruled your country for four hundred years and taught you how to cook."

Nico clenched the table with his beefy hands, his knuckles turning white. He pushed himself up to tower over the table. His dark chocolate eyes grew wide while the nostrils of his broad flat nose flared.

"What did you say?" his voice thundered. He picked up the plate in front of him and flung it to the teak deck. Crash! "That's what I think of *your* Turkish food."

Chloe started to speak. I grabbed her arm and shook my head. We would charge them for the broken plates. I knew better than to get involved.

The Turkish woman clasped the blue-eyed glass bauble hanging from her neck. Fire seemed to shoot out of her eyes toward the man. She then muttered something in Turkish, rose from her chair, and shook her gnarled finger at Nico. "May you be shot with greasy bullets," she uttered, raising both hands above her head.

Chloe's eyes went wide and she whispered, "Did she just put a curse on him?"

"I think so."

We backed away from the table.

"I thought they were friends," Chloe said.

"Not any more." We retreated into the galley to the sound of more plates breaking. Patrick came wheeling in a few minutes later.

"What's happening out there?"

I laid a hand on his arm, hoping I could convince him not to go investigate. "Just leave them," I said. "It'll be okay. We'll replace the dishes in Spain."

Patrick clenched his jaw. "Make it stop or I will." He stormed out of the galley and down the corridor.

The cacophony reverberated from the aft deck, down the passageway. The fight blared on. Chloe and I hid, refusing to go out and serve dessert until it was over. One by one, the crew came into the galley to see what the commotion was about.

"Some end to the season," I said.

"You better hope dessert goes over better than lunch," Dylan said. "I'm not going to be able to get that syrup out of the teak." He pointed to my dessert.

I looked at the *baklava*, a dish I knew both Turkish and Greek cultures claimed as their own. I'd planned on serving it for dessert, but thought twice about adding to the conflict. I didn't want the woman putting a curse on me, too. We had enough problems on the boat without a crazy Turkish curse being thrown into the mix.

"Maybe a bowl of figs would be a better idea." I said to Chloe.

Just as I was convinced my choice for lunch had kicked off another hundred-year war, Stoyan walked into the galley and grabbed a skewer. He dipped it in the yogurt mixture.

"My favorite." He ripped into the lamb and spoke with his mouth full. "My grandmother used to make this for me."

I was confused. Stoyan was from Bulgaria. Maybe she crossed the border to marry. "Was she Greek or Turkish?"

"Nah," he scoffed, taking another bite and holding up the bowl of yogurt. "This is *snezhanka*." He said between mouthfuls. "Is Bulgarian food!"

Turkish Lamb Kebabs with Greek Tsatziki

3 pounds lamb tenderloin
2 cloves garlic, minced
1/4 cup olive oil
1 tablespoon tomato paste
1 tablespoon pomegranate molasses
1 tablespoon ground cumin
1 tablespoon dried mint
1 tablespoon dried oregano
1 teaspoon sweet paprika
1 teaspoon hot paprika
1 teaspoon sea salt

Slice lamb into one-inch cubes and marinate in the rest of the ingredients for 4 hours. Soak 18 ten-inch skewers in water to prevent burning on the grill. Thread pieces of lamb on a skewer, leaving little space between the cubes and enough room on one end to grasp the skewer.

Grill the skewers, over medium-high heat, turning over once, for 6-8 minutes until medium-rare. Transfer skewers to a platter and cover with foil to keep warm.

Tsatziki Sauce:
1 English cucumber
1 clove garlic, minced
2 tablespoons white wine vinegar
1 shallot, minced
2 tablespoons dill, chopped
2-1/2 cups Greek yogurt
2 tablespoons olive oil
1 lemon, juiced
1/2 teaspoon sea salt
12 grinds black pepper

Peel and grate the cucumber. Mix all together and serve chilled.

Serve with: Flatbreads, black olives, shredded lettuce and chopped tomatoes

Serves 6

This is Greece!

*T*he last of our guests left, our season ended, and Patrick gave the crew the first three days off to explore Athens. He and I covered watching the boat while they had fun. The first day we spent almost totally sleeping. You could have rolled a bowling ball down the crew hallway and not hit anybody. It had been a long and hectic season. The crew deserved some relaxation.

Day two, brought a few faces out of hiding, and by the third day, everyone was back to normal. For the most part, they headed to the bar or on a sight-seeing afternoon to the Acropolis. Tom was the only one who hung back to call Katie on Skype.

"How is she?" I asked when he finished. I wasn't sure about revealing I knew about him and Gwen. Throughout the remainder of the summer, they had sat next to each other during meal times and scheduled their breaks to coincide. They both worked the late shift and would be alone together after we all went to bed. I had tried not to say anything, but it was hard not to notice what was going on.

He looked down at his feet. "Not so good." He kicked at an imaginary rock on the floor. "We broke up."

"Oh, I'm sorry Tom." I laid my hand on his arm. "I liked Katie."

He nodded.

"It's tough being away." I said. "You're off having these awesome adventures with other people..." I trailed off.

Tom nodded. "She didn't want me to come." He scratched at the back of his head. "She wanted to get married. I didn't."

I nodded.

"She's met someone who wants to marry her."

I wasn't so much surprised at the statement as the timing. Katie was a beautiful girl, bright and fun to be around, but Tom had only joined us two months earlier. This was quick.

"I'm sorry, Tom."

I knew yachting could be lonely and hard on a single person. But he was perfect for yachting. His bright personality and natural abilities made him a great crewmember. One day, I predicted, he would be captaining his own yacht.

"Does this mean you'll stay with us?"

"If Patrick wants me to."

I didn't like to speak for Patrick, but I was pretty sure this was okay.

"Of course!" I gave him a hug. "We're going to have so much fun this year. It will be completely different from last year in the Bahamas."

Tom laughed. "Yeah, how did we get through that?"

I shook my head. "I have no idea." I laughed, thinking of all that happened then and now on this new boat. "I'm not even sure how we got through this." But, we had, and, as always, we were headed to a new destination for a shipyard period before continuing with the adventure.

* * * *

"Are we there yet?" I asked, excited. We were racing from the crowded town of Oia to the fishing village of Ammoundi to taste the local grilled octopus we'd fallen in love with all over Greece.

"Almost." Patrick was giddy with excitement too.

The crew had returned from their three days off and were now responsible for watching the boat while we explored. Patrick booked us a flight to Santorini and reservations at a small hotel imbedded in the rocks overlooking the Aegean Sea. We spent the first night weaving the narrow jam-packed streets of Oia. People were everywhere. Each shop overflowed with tourists. Each restaurant had a waiting list. It was crazy and not the relaxing getaway Patrick had envisioned. We skipped dinner that night and fell straight to sleep, a shaft of moonlight streaming through our bedroom window.

The next morning, we made our way down a steep, winding path to the fishing village below. Hardly noticing, we passed the blue-domes and whitewashed walls of the buildings nestled into the side of a sunken volcano. The dramatic view over the caldera was lost on me. I could see nothing but the narrow steep steps under my feet as we descended. We reached the bottom and collapsed into the plastic chairs of the first tavern we came to. My stomach growled. A man with shoulder-length dark curls approached with bottles of water in his hand.

Without delay, we ordered Mythos beers, a plate of octopus, another of calamari, and an eggplant salad.

The man returned with our meal. Famished, we ravaged the plates in quick succession. The octopus disappeared in seconds. I don't even remember the calamari, it was gone so fast. I took a breath and leaned back from the table.

"Mmm," was all Patrick could muster, his mouth full of charred tentacles.

The blistering Mediterranean sun blazed down, scorching my skin. Small wooden fishing boats painted bright red and green bobbed in the sapphire water. Rhythmic waves flooded the pebbled beach. It was quiet and peaceful, in stark contrast to the crazed mob overhead.

"Well captain," I finally spoke after the feast. "Not such a bad spot to retreat to."

Patrick leaned back in his chair and looked out over the fishing boats. "No, there are worse places to be stuck on a day off."

I leaned over the table and kissed Patrick. "Even in the worst of places, I love being stuck with you."

"Good." He laughed. "Because, that's what you are." He kissed me back. "Stuck."

I shrugged, not feeling as stuck right then and there as I did when we were onboard and in the middle of chaos. I thought about the crazyness of the last year and realized, even when it spiraled out of our control, I still loved this life and couldn't imagine doing anything else. I raised my glass in a toast. "To a good life."

He smiled. "A damn good life."

Relaxed this time, I picked up my fork to taste the eggplant salad. It was juicy and smooth in my mouth. I took another forkful to be sure. It wasn't bitter or biting as eggplant can be. This was sweet and velvety smooth.

"Yum." The sentiment escaped my lips.

The waiter returned with more beers in hand. "This is good, no?" I nodded and he started to explain. "We use white aubergines, from the fire." He pointed to the wood-burning grill our octopus had come from.

"They're sweet." I said.

He smiled; the whiteness of his teeth showed bright against the dark olive-tone of his skin. "They grow like this, with the earth of the volcano."

"You don't add anything else?" I thought there had to be sugar.

"Of course! This is Greece!" He shook his head and laughed. "Lemon and olive oil, always." Still laughing, he retreated back inside the tavern.

I looked over my shoulder, skyward. The crowds were gathering above to watch the sunset.

"How about another dish of that salad?" I asked Patrick, unwilling to leave our sanctuary and join the mob.

He nodded and smiled slyly. "And one more octopus?"

"Of course!" I laughed. "This is Greece!"

Santorini Eggplant Salad

6 cloves garlic, unpeeled
2 white eggplants (you can use the black eggplant but the taste will be slightly sharper)
1 onion, unpeeled
1 teaspoon sea salt
1 lemon, juiced
1/4 cup olive oil
1/2 teaspoon sea salt
1/4 teaspoon black pepper

Wrap the cloves of garlic in an aluminum foil package. Prick the skin of the eggplant and roast in a 400 degree oven with the onion and the garlic cloves for half an hour until they are all soft. Cool and peel the garlic and onion. Peel the eggplant and place in a colander. Sprinkle with 1 teaspoon sea salt. Gently mash the eggplant with a potato masher to press out the juices. Drain for 20 minutes. Place everything in a processor and blend for 10 seconds until slightly smooth texture is achieved.

Taste for seasoning and serve with cucumber slices, feta cheese, kalamata olives and pita breads.

Serves 6

A Regrouping

*B*y the time we secured the lines and straightened the fenders, it was already late, but Spain doesn't even consider eating until long after the sun has retired for the evening. Famished after the long crossing from Greece, Patrick and I wandered through the old Roman streets of Barcelona, dizzy with hunger. The rest of the crew had opted for the nearest bar, but we set out in search of food. Patrick was the captain, and we knew the crew would have a better time without us there. No matter how cool and fun he was, no one wanted to party with the boss around.

"Have a good time," Patrick said as they headed out the door.

"Sure you won't come?" Tom asked.

He stood behind Gwen with his arm around her waist. During the past month they had gone from a late night hookup to something more.

"Thanks, no." Patrick replied. "We're just going to grab some dinner." He turned to Anna who was on watch. "We won't be long. I have my cell if there are any problems." He thought for a second. "You can join everyone else when we get back."

Anna smiled. "That's okay. I want to get some sleep so I can go see the Gaudi exhibits tomorrow."

It felt good to be back in the shipyard. The summer had been hectic. We'd been thrown in once again at the last minute and had little time to think. Now was our time to regroup. Over the next few weeks we would work a normal schedule of eight to five and all rotate through vacations. It would be quiet and peaceful; the calm before the next storm.

* * * *

We passed stone buildings with more history than I could ever remember, to a tiny square where tapas bars crowded every corner. In the one we chose, dark-haired men stood behind a long counter, backs to us, hunkered over a stove. They were busy submerging squid in oil and tossing tiny green peppers in a smoking-hot, cast-iron pan. We pulled bar stools up to the high counter and watched the action of the cooks like we were following a soccer match. Our necks craned to see a plate of sausage and beans being delivered to a couple across the room. Razor clams sizzled on hot skillets. A *tortilla* passed so close we could have reached out and taken a bite. We followed it with our eyes.

A round of steaming clams was set just to the right of us; their smell filled the small space. We immediately ordered a bowl and watched as one of the cooks with a heavy pan flicked his wrist, sending a dozen muscles and their juices flying through the air. He caught the wave of shellfish and broth without spilling a drop.

Without a word, he placed the bowl in front of us.

With my first bite, I fell in love with Spain.

"So," I started, not sure where I was heading. "What do you think?"

Patrick looked up from his plate of chorizo and chickpeas. "About the season or the shipyard period?"

"Both."

"Well." Patrick took another bite. "I like the boat and the crew. After a rough start, it all worked out great."

I nodded. I, too, loved the crew and the boat. "It sounds like there's a *but* coming."

Patrick nodded slowly. "European boats are different from what we're used to."

"How so?"

Other than the places we visited, I hadn't noticed a difference from any other boat we worked on. In fact, I thought this was a better boat than the last. It wasn't breaking every week like our boat in the Bahamas the past winter. Granted, we had Stoyan to prevent any major problems and fix those that did occur, but all in all the boat ran like a Swiss watch all season. All the drama had occurred with the crew.

"There's no winter season in Europe." Patrick played with the last of the food on his plate. "It's too cold to travel anywhere."

I knew all this. We'd come to Spain to sit for the winter and wouldn't have guests again until May. The time alone would give us the chance to restock and clean everything from top to bottom. There would be engine maintenance, touch-ups on paint, and restocking supplies. We had a chance to get to things that we had no time to think about during the season.

"Seven months is a long time." Patrick looked at me. "Do you think we'll get bored?"

I hadn't thought of it that way. I was just excited to wake up tomorrow at a civilized hour and not have to bake bread. I thought of the back-to-back charters we'd done all summer long and the miles we covered from Italy to France to Greece and Spain. We had lost our first mate within two weeks of starting on the boat, our new first mate had been propositioned by a guest, Tom and Gwen started sleeping together, and the Greek family smashed all my favorite dishes. We worked ninety-two days straight and served one hundred and eighty-six meals. Hell, I was exhausted just remembering.

"Let's just enjoy this while it lasts."

* * * *

We stumbled out of the tapas bar, full of flavor. The waistband of my jeans cut tight into my belly, bloated with Spanish fare. The narrow streets of the Gothic district had filled with people while we were inside. On the corner, a group of musicians performed in front of an open guitar case. As one dark, brooding man played guitar, another clapped his hands in a muffled rhythm. A woman dressed in a low-cut red dress twirled the ruffles of her skirt while pounding her feet to the beat. Her severe expression and the slamming of her heels portrayed the passion of Flamenco to the gathering crowd. We stopped to watch, mesmerized by the show.

The bells of Santa Maria del Mar rang, filling the night with a haunting melody that added to the air of the Gothic district. We passed bars that exploded onto the dark narrow street with warm golden light and laughter. Fashionably dressed couples hurried past. The Barcelona night vibrated with activity.

"Hey Pat," a voice called from the patio across the street.

Patrick scanned the crowd, confused. We'd just arrived in port, and he didn't know anyone here. His eyes settled on John, a captain we knew from Australia.

"Hey!" Patrick's eyes lit with joy. "What're you doing here?" Patrick grabbed my hand, looked both ways, and pulled me across the street toward the bar.

"Come, join us." John was sitting with half a dozen other people. He stood and scanned the area for empty chairs.

We threaded through the maze of people to the table and were introduced to six other captains. A woman came by to take our order. Following the preset of the table, we ordered another round of Estrella beers.

"Boat's in for a paint job," John said as he took a long pull from his bottle. "When did you get here?"

Patrick looked at his watch. "About two hours ago."

Terry, the captain of the boat beside us, held up his bottle in toast. "Welcome to the end of the season then."

Patrick laughed and leaned back in his chair. "Yeah, it was some hell of a season."

He peeled the label off his beer bottle as he told the story of our maiden voyage, and Nick's drunken disappearing act. Whether because the season was over, or the fact that he was surrounded by other captains, Patrick relaxed and laughed at the absurdity of it all. Years seemed to drain from his face as he told our stories.

"That's nothing, mate," John said. "I just had a trip of recovering alcoholics we served rum punches to." Everyone at the table laughed.

The captain beside John nodded his head. "Well, our stewardess came home from the night before, still in her dolled-up tarty outfit, make-up half way down her face." He held his hand mid-cheek to indicate just how far the make-up had run. "Breasts hanging out to here." He cupped his hands far in front of him like carrying bags of groceries. "And walked onto the back of the boat, past the owners who were sitting having breakfast."

That brought on an even bigger laugh and more nods of understanding. Patrick laughed harder than I'd seen him do all summer.

Jeff chimed in from the other end of the table. "I caught our deckhand in the Jacuzzi with two girls from the bar while our owners were on board." He held his hands up in a shrug. "I wasn't sure if I should punish him or cheer him on."

"Hell, at least he wasn't pissing where he ate. I've gone through four stews this season alone." John signaled the server for another round of beers. "The first mate keeps shagging them, and when he finally tells them about his wife and children back home, they leave." John shook his head. "I've had to make his family tree part of my interview process."

Patrick's eyes twinkled. "Did you fire him?"

"Nah, the owner would have been proud had he caught him."

Terry smirked and added, "Our owner fired my chief stew half-way through a trip this year."

"What happened?" I asked.

"She was in the middle of serving dinner and went down to the laundry room for a dish towel. The handle fell off the door, locking her inside. The rest of the crew were watching a movie and couldn't hear her calling for help. No one knew what had happened, and when she didn't return to the table after forty-five minutes, the owner got pissed and screamed at me to fire her."

"But, it wasn't her fault," I said.

I remembered when I first started cooking in a restaurant and was stuck in the walk-in for twenty minutes because I couldn't figure out how to open the self-shutting door. I still shuddered at the memory, embarrassed, but didn't think that was any more a fireable offense than the handle falling off during dinner.

"I know, but the owner wouldn't listen. We had to hide her for the rest of the trip until he calmed down."

"Ha!" Paul choked on his beer, hurrying to swallow to tell us his tale. "I was fired by the six-year-old grandson because we didn't have his favorite brand of apple juice on board."

John laughed and turned to Patrick. "See, mate, you had it easy." He clapped Patrick on the shoulder. "It could've been worse." He smiled like Lucifer. "A lot worse."

Clams with Sherry and Iberico Ham

2 pounds fresh clams
2 tablespoons coarse sea salt
6 cups cold water

2 tablespoons olive oil
4 cloves garlic, minced
2 shallots, finely chopped
1/4 cup Iberico ham, finely chopped (or Serrano ham)
1/4 cup dry sherry
2 tablespoons parsley, chopped

Scrub clams and soak them in water and coarse salt for 45 minutes. Discard any that are open.

Heat a heavy-bottomed sauté pan over high heat. Add olive oil, Iberico ham, onions, and garlic. Sauté 3 minutes until the onions are soft. Drain the clams and add to the pot with sherry. Cover and cook for 4 minutes until the shells have opened. Discard any that remain closed.

Toss with parsley and ladle into bowls.

Serve with crusty bread, rubbed with tomato and drizzled in olive oil, and a glass of wine.

Serves 4

Loco

*T*he weather turned cold and rainy that month in Barcelona—a dreary signal that summer had receded. The sun began rising a little later and dropping a little earlier. I woke in the morning to darkness and stumbled to the market in a haze. I didn't begin to smile until the smell of *café solo* hit me.

"*Hola Guapo*," Armando, the barista, greeted me.

I smiled at his use of the slang "Hey good looking." Wrinkled, dowdy old men with sour faces and poor dental hygiene surrounded us. "*Café solo*?" He raised his bushy dark eyebrow in question, but had already started my morning coffee. I had the same each day.

"*Si y una tortilla por favor.*" It was the little Spanish I knew. I'm much better speaking food in a different language than with conversation, and tortilla had been a favorite long before I set foot on the shores of this country.

Armando brought me the strong shot of coffee, grabbed my hand, and pressed a package of sugar into my palm.

"For sweetness," he said with an unparalleled seriousness, like I may have forgotten since yesterday.

His apron barely concealed the dark curls of his chest as he leaned over the counter. He smelled of musk and cigarettes.

I tipped my head and threw back the first jolt of caffeine. I shuddered and ordered another. Armando laughed, a guttural sound from deep within him.

The *tortilla* was simple—eggs and potatoes, a staple on tapas menus of the region. Armando sliced chewy bread and rubbed a half tomato on top, spreading its sweet flavor over the surface. He picked up a slender bottle of olive oil and drizzled a golden sheen on top. The bread glistened. Armando leaned in close and pinched sea salt between his thick fingers. He sprinkled it over the bread like an artist applying the finishing touch to his masterpiece.

He stood watchful, guarding my first bite. The creamy interior of the silken egg and soft potato melted in my mouth. Each forkful was smoother than the last. The bread crunched between my teeth. The fruitiness of the olive oil enveloped my senses.

I smiled and racked my brain for a way to communicate just how perfect the meal was. *Bueno* was the only word I could think of. "*Me gusto,*" I said. I like. I smiled again, hoping he understood.

Armando's face was solemn. He bowed deeply from the waist like a knight before the Queen. "*De nada.*" It's nothing.

I ventured out into the market in search of the day's lunch. With only crew on the boat now, I had more time to explore the market. Instead of the mad dash to procure and get back to the galley, I could wander and discover all this Spanish market had to offer.

Like wind chimes, legs of ham hung from the ceiling in front of me; the black hoof of the pig still attached.

"*Iberico?*" I asked.

"*Si,*" the man behind the counter said. I knew a little about these already. The wild pigs grazed on acorns in the forest, so their meat was nutty and sweet. They were cured and hung for up to three years. During my first foray to this market, I picked up a whole leg and brought it back to the boat.

Stoyan entered the galley as I set up the rack to hold the leg. Like a torturer's contraption it held the hoof in place high above the counter with a metal screw while the rest of the leg hung on an angle, resting on the wooden surface below. Stoyan picked up my carving knife and began to shave thin strips from the leg.

"Good shit," he said as he carved more slices for Patrick.

"Mmm," Patrick said between bites. "This is good shit."

"For lunch today," Stoyan said. "With bread, a little tomato, and cheese. No more."

"Sounds good to me." I liked when crew made requests. It meant I didn't have to think, and they got exactly what they liked.

At noon that day, I placed the rack in the center of the table along with a salad and a platter of cheeses and tomatoes. Stoyan took charge and shaved *Iberico* ham for the whole table. The sweet and concentrated flavor danced on my tongue. The rich fat flavored my mouth as it slid down my throat. It was a simple lunch with a wallop of flavor. I could get used to eating like this.

By the end of the week, the leg had vanished, and I was back in the market looking for a replacement.

* * * *

I wandered past skinned rabbits, their eyes bulging from the heads. A baby lamb sat propped up in one stall, its front legs sprawled to balance the body. Except for the fact it had been shorn, the lamb looked as though it was resting under the shade of a tree. Large grey tongues of cows were piled on top of each other beside a tangle of white, lacy stomachs. Soft, squishy livers glistened inside the case. Chickens lay with their heads at crazy angles, their necks broken, but not removed. This was a long way from the plastic, sterile looking grocery aisles of home.

I passed tables blooming with Valencia oranges and oak casks piled high with salty *marcona* almonds. Fish that looked like they had been run over by a car and squished flat lay on ice beside the hook-like curls of orange-pink langoustines.

I wandered over to the cheese counter where a robust woman with dark curls stood slicing wedges of nutty *Manchego*.

"*Hola.*" She had a singsong voice.

All of the sudden, I was stuck. Food shopping in a market is usually the easiest thing to do in a different language. Point and hold up your fingers. How hard could it be? But, I wanted to know what specific cheeses I was buying for lunch that day. Were they cow's milk cheeses from the north, or sheep's milk from the plains? Part of traveling as a chef was to learn about the food in different countries, but often the language barrier got in the way.

I pointed to a snowy white log, assuming it was a goat cheese from the Mediterranean region. "*Que?*"

My red-hair and pale white skin must have alerted the woman to the fact I wasn't a native Spaniard. She screwed her face to one side and thought a moment.

Suddenly, her eyes sparked to life. She raised her index fingers to the sides of her temples and wiggled them. "Nay, nay," she brayed. She raised her button black eyes to make sure I understood.

I laughed, knowing it was goat's milk cheese, and moved to the next one in the case. It was a breast-shaped dome. To this the woman began moving her jaw in an exaggerated chewing motion. "Moo, moo," she said, laughing with delight.

She was really getting into this game. She picked up a hard wedge of cured cheese that was cracked and dry. Her voice became higher in pitch as she pursed her lips together and bleated out the sound of a sheep.

I couldn't help laughing. It was a crazy sight. By now, the grumpy men from the café had gathered around us. At first, they eyed us suspiciously and shook their heads, but soon they too were joining in the barnyard song. A man with the deep wrinkles of a dried apple head doll began prancing around the stall and wiggling his fingers under his chin like a Billy goat. His amigos cheered him on. The woman behind the counter laughed and pulled another goat's milk cheese from the display for me.

By the end of the show, I had a variety of Spanish cheeses to fill my bag and a pretty good idea of what they were. I could now speak a few more words of Spanish, as long as they were to the tune of *Old MacDonald's Farm*.

Tortilla

1 cup olive oil
1 yellow onion, sliced thin
2 cloves garlic, sliced thin
4 potatoes. peeled and cut crosswise into ½" thick slices
1 teaspoon sea salt
6 eggs

In a 12" skillet with sloped sides, heat the olive oil over high heat. Sauté the onions and garlic for one minute, until soft. Add the potatoes and sauté for 15 minutes until the potatoes are soft. Drain the oil from the potatoes, reserving the oil for a later use. Add half the sea salt. Whisk the eggs in a large bowl with the remaining sea salt. Add the potatoes and rest for 2 minutes for potatoes to "absorb" some of the egg mixture.

Pre-heat oven to 325 degrees.

Return the pan to the stove and heat over medium high heat. Brush some of the drained olive oil in the pan to prevent sticking. Pour the egg mixture into the pan. Shake vigorously for 30 seconds to create a soft fluffy tortilla. Continue cooking for 3 minutes. When the edges are set, place skillet in the oven for 10 minutes until the top is set. Remove and cool for 2 minutes. Shake the pan once to loosen the tortilla. When it slides around in the pan easily, flip the tortilla by placing a plate over the skillet and inverting both at the same time.

Cut into wedges. Serve warm or at room temperature.

Serve at anytime of the day—in the morning with bread and coffee, in the afternoon with salad and a glass of wine, or at night with cheese

Serves 8

Marrakech Meanderings

*I*t was our turn for a holiday. We rotated the vacation schedule so that everyone could disappear for a few weeks before we ramped up again. We had discussed trekking in Peru or surfing in Bali, but Patrick's responsibility won out, and we opted for a destination closer to the boat in case something went wrong. Morocco was only a short flight, but a world away, from anywhere we'd traveled.

The narrow streets of Marrakech's medina tangled like spaghetti, leading to the heart of the city. The souq, an Arabic market was where we were headed. Saffron yellow, burnt-red and tan spices mounded in barrels along the way. Mule carts laden with bundles of fresh mint, coriander, and parsley were parked along the side of the street.

"Look. Just look." Arabian men sat in front of endless stalls calling to us like auctioneers, bidding us to enter their shops. "Ali Baba, come look." Patrick's blond beard evoked the nickname called to him everywhere. It stood out as much as the red hair I tucked behind a scarf. No amount of discretion in this Muslim country would hide the fact we were two pale-skinned people among a darker race.

Our foray into the labyrinth had meaning. We had a destination. The problem was, we were hopelessly lost.

"This way." Patrick led me down an alleyway and around three right turns to a dead end. We doubled back to where we started.

"Maybe we should have turned left at the hanging lantern store?" I was only guessing. We'd passed four identical shops with intricate tin lanterns and candles with stretched goatskin and hennaed designs hanging from the ceiling. I had no idea which one marked the correct place to turn.

Patrick sighed loudly and turned back the way we came.

"Ali Baba, where are you going?" A man asked. After an hour of trying to find the correct passage, we resigned ourselves to asking for help.

"*Mechoui?*" Patrick hesitated, not sure he was pronouncing it right.

"Yes, come," he said.

We shrugged off the anxiety of being lost and gave ourselves over to the guide.

Hazzid had the soft features of a Berber man. His dark tight curls were trimmed close to the scalp, his skin a latte color. His dress of black jeans and Western jacket told the all too familiar tale of a man who left the mountain village to work in the larger city of Marrakech. He wove us down serpentine alleyways and around corners. He walked fast, glancing back to make sure we followed close.

"Watch, Victoria. Watch here." He pointed out every misplaced stone that maimed the street, caring for me as he would his own child.

The hot, smoky smell of roasted meat told us he'd found the place. A row of tables heaving with cuts of lamb spread out in front of us. Eyes stared at us from roasted sockets as we passed the first stall. The second table was identical to the first, a mountain of legs, ribs, and rumps. The scent of cumin followed us from stall to stall.

Finally, we stopped. "My family." Hazzid introduced us to two men in white chef's jackets, their bellies stained with grease.

"*La bes,*" I ventured a Berber greeting. They laughed.

"Hello. Big welcome." Smiles erupted on their faces.

Hazzid stepped behind his brothers and lifted a round stone from the floor. "Victoria, look." This time he wasn't cautioning me. He showed me how the lamb was cooked. Through the manhole, a pit was dug deep under the street. In the center of the chamber embers of a long-burning fire glowed, lighting the space. A dozen lamb carcasses hung from hooks above the coals. Heavily scented smoke clouded the space, permeating the meat with its flavor. The earth-oven had cooked the lamb slowly, for hours, melting away fat and leaving moist, tender meat.

"*Mechoui*," Hazzid stated as way of an explanation.

"You try?" One of the men asked.

"Yes, please."

He raised a large cleaver. With one stoke he split the lamb through the backbone. Another blow sectioned off a hunk for us. Tendrils of steam rose from the chopping process. Using the knife and his free hand, he scraped and scooped the meat onto one side of a scale. On the other, he stacked weights.

"One kilo. Good for you." He heaped more meat than I could imagine eating in one sitting onto a paper plate and loaded the top with two rounds of Moroccan pita bread. I reached for the plate, but Hazzid quickly grabbed it from me. Clearly, he was now our official host. He carried the meat up the stairs to the open-air terrace above the stall.

Over the building tops, the Atlas Mountains loomed clear and bright. "My home." Hazzid smiled proudly and retreated back to speak with his family.

We wasted no time. Soft pieces of meat fell from the bones. Custom dictated we eat only with our right hand—something that proved harder than mastering chopsticks. We dipped the meat into dishes of cumin salt. Succulent flavor filled my mouth and coated the inside with silk. Hot juice glistened on my fingers. Patrick groaned. This was good. We devoured the whole plate, and I wondered if Muslim customs would frown on a woman sucking the bones in public. It took a great deal of inner strength to resist the urge.

Hazzid returned with a tray of tea. He held the ornate silver teapot at a great height, pouring clear brown liquid in an elaborate show of service into the tiny glasses below. The high pour brought new aromas to the air. Fresh mint replaced the smell of roasted lamb, making my mouth water again.

Hazzid held his cup high. "Big welcome."

Later, we meandered the streets, our bellies pregnant with the flavor of Morocco, no longer worried about being lost.

* * * *

After such a big meal the day before, I lounged in the courtyard of our Riad most of the morning, enjoying the peace. Patrick reclined on a chaise, reading. We would be back onboard and thrown into the latest drama soon enough. On that day we just wanted quiet solace.

Sultry African sunlight streamed through the branches of an orange tree, casting shadows like a paper doily on my skin. The soothing sound of water bubbled from the fountain and the serenity of the abode was in stark contrast to the chaos of the market we'd been in yesterday, and miles away from the college-dorm-like atmosphere of the boat.

I could've spent every meal in Morocco at that market. Cauldrons of snails bubbled in broth, sending a woodsy aroma through the air. Roasted sheep's heads lay in wait of adventurous eaters. Carts heaped with dates, apricots, and figs sat beside mountains of almonds and walnuts. Snake charmers lulled both serpent and audience with haunting melodies, while fire-eaters rallied the crowds with daredevil performances. Almond-eyed boys led monkeys through the square and the small hennaed hands of young girls begged for coins. The market was alive with mystery.

But I wanted more than to taste the spiced foods of Marrakesh. I wanted to learn to make them. That's where Abdelwahed, the cook at the Riad, came in.

"Are you ready to learn Moroccan food?" His voice, though soft and reserved, startled me out of my bliss.

"Only if you promise I'll be able to recreate something as tasty as we've had all weekend."

His thin angular face broke into a smile. "As you wish." He bowed low, raising a hand to his head to catch the paper chef's hat as it fell. He sounded like a genie from the Arabian Nights tales. He waved his hand indicating I should enter the kitchen before him.

"Today, I make you *tagine*."

Laid out on the spotless countertop was a single clay tagine pot and a mortar and pestle. Bunches of jade green herbs were piled in the corner. Six small glass dishes held spices the color of bricks. A chicken sat chopped into pieces on a wooden cutting board. This was the sparsest classroom I'd seen.

"Sounds divine." I was already lulled into an exotic mood by the crimson color of the cupboards in the kitchen and the golden trim.

"Most of our dishes are made in a tagine." He pointed to the dish on the counter. "Many homes do not have ovens, so the women cook their food over a fire." He lifted the conical shaped lid. "This works like an oven but keeps everything moist."

Abdelwahed grabbed the cilantro and parsley and began pounding them in the mortar while he spoke. "All the flavor you put into the tagine goes onto the plate." He picked up a soft spongy lemon. "These are preserved lemons. They go into the *charmoula* we use with the chicken." He peeled away the bright yellow rind and added the flesh to the herbs.

I knew a little about Moroccan food and knew I loved these lemons. I made them on the boat, covering them with sea salt for three weeks to marinate and mellow. "How long do you preserve them?"

"A year," he said.

And that summed up my whole love of travel; what I thought I knew was often wrong. And that's why I was there; to learn from the source.

Abdelwahed picked up the glass bowls of spices. He dipped an antique spoon into khaki colored cumin and crimson paprika and sprinkled them over the herb and lemon mixture. He pounded some more, producing a paste that filled the tiny kitchen with its warm smell.

He placed the bottom of the tagine on the gas-stove top and sprinkled more spices over the chicken, turning the medallions to rust. "This is *ras al hanout*. It's a blend of thirty-seven spices."

My eyes widened in surprise. "Thirty-seven? Wow!"

"It's what you call curry powder."

Abdelwahed swirled olive oil into the tagine and placed the chicken inside to sear. After thirty seconds, he flipped the pieces over and spooned the *charmoula* over the pieces. He placed the lid on the tagine and transferred the rest of the paste to a small dish decorated in a Moroccan design. "You'll make this on the boat?"

"I will now." I nodded, while my mind swirled like the steam rising from the tagine. This dish would work well for a lunch, combined with a few different salads and pastries. "It will be my reminder of Morocco and my time in your kitchen."

Abdelwahed bowed. "It would be my honor to have my red kitchen remembered by you."

Five minutes later, he lifted the lid of the tagine. Steam mushroomed out. He sprinkled slivers of preserved lemon peel over the chicken. He placed it in front of me and bowed again. "*Bon appetit.*"

I dipped my fork into the sauce and popped it in my mouth. It was soft and smooth instead of acidic like fresh lemons. Mellow spices mingled together, none overpowering the other. The moist chicken slipped down my throat. I smiled. This was worth staying home from the market for.

Mechoui

This is a long slow roast so the meat is moist and falling-off-the-bone tender. Allow for 8 hours cooking before serving.

1 leg of lamb, 7 pounds with bone
4 tablespoons olive oil
8 cloves garlic, minced
2 teaspoons sea salt
24 grinds of black pepper
2 teaspoons cumin
1 teaspoon turmeric

2 tablespoons sea salt
1 tablespoon cumin

flat breads, such as naan or pitas
Greek yogurt
Shredded lettuce
Diced tomatoes

Preheat oven to 250 degrees.

Make a dozen or more cuts deep into the meat with the tip of a sharp knife. Combine the olive oil with the garlic and spices. Spread the mixture over the entire leg of lamb. Use your finger to work the mix into the incisions made with the knife. Place the leg of lamb in a roasting pan.

Cover the lamb with foil, sealing the edges tightly. Roast the lamb for 7-1/2 hours. Unwrap and baste every hour after the first 3 hours cooking. Reseal the foil each time,

Remove the foil and increase the oven temperature to 450 degrees. Brown the lamb for 20 minutes. Let lamb rest for 20 minutes.

Shred lamb off the bone and transfer to a platter. Pour the pan juices over the lamb. Combine cumin and sea salt and place in a small dish on the platter for sprinkling over meat.

Have everyone wrap warm lamb, shredded lettuce and diced tomatoes in warm flatbread smeared with Greek yogurt. Sprinkle cumin salt over top and roll like a wrap to eat.

Serves 8

Chicken Tagine
with Preserved Lemons and Olives

Charmoula:
1/4 cup cilantro
1/4 cup parsley
4 cloves garlic
1 preserved lemon, pulp only, reserve the peel for garnish (or juice of 2 lemons and 1 ½ teaspoons sea salt)
1 teaspoon cumin
1 teaspoon paprika
1 pinch of saffron
16 grinds black pepper
1/4 cup olive oil

12 skinless chicken thighs

Rinse the preserved lemon under cool running water to minimize the salt in the dish. Peel the lemon and reserve the peel for garnish. In a food processor, combine all the ingredients. Process until a rough paste is achieved. Rub into chicken thighs and leave to marinate for 20 minutes.

3 tablespoons olive oil
2 onions, finely sliced
4 cloves garlic, sliced in quarters
2" piece fresh ginger, grated
1 cinnamon stick
2 cups chicken stock
24 green Queen olives, pitted
18 kalamata olives, pitted
1 tablespoon parsley, chopped
1 tablespoon cilantro, chopped

In a heavy-bottomed pot heat the oil over medium-high heat and sauté onions and garlic for 5 minutes. Stir in ginger and cinnamon stick.
Nestle the chicken thighs into the onions and scrape all of the marinade out of the bowl. Add the chicken stock. Reduce heat to medium-low. Simmer, covered for 20 minutes, turning the chicken over once halfway through. Julienne the reserved peel and add it to the chopped parsley and cilantro; set aside. Add the olives to the chicken. Simmer, uncovered for 5-10 minutes until the sauce is thick. Taste for seasoning. Garnish with cilantro, parsley and lemon peel mixture and serve with couscous.

Serves 6

~Continued on next page

Preserved Lemons:

These can be purchased in jars, but are so much more flavorful if made from scratch. I keep a container in my fridge at all times and frequently use them as a substitute for fresh lemons in salads, fish dishes, and sauces.

4 lemons
1 cup coarse sea salt
4 lemons, juiced

Wash the lemons and cut them in half. Place in a container completely covered with sea salt. Squeeze the juice of the second 4 lemons over top, being careful not to expose any part of the lemon. Add more salt if needed to completely cover.

Place in the refrigerator for 1 month (the longer they are left the better).

To use: rinse the lemon peel under the tap to remove the salt.
Preserved lemons will last up to a year in the fridge.

Cous-cous:
3 cups chicken stock
2 cups cous-cous

Bring the chicken stock to a boil in a sauce pan. Add cous-cous, cover and remove from heat. Allow to sit for 5 minutes. Use a fork to fluff the grains.

Bored on Board

*P*atrick was right. I was bored. We'd been in Barcelona for three months. I can't say I was sad, because the time off gave me an opportunity to explore more of Spain, but it also meant I had little more to do each day than cook lunch and dinner for the crew. After cleaning out the walk-in, the pantry, and the hood fan, I still had many more hours to fill. My morning forays to the market only lasted until nine.

Each day I made a large, elaborate lunch for the crew. We had adopted the European-style of having our main meal during the day and then snacking on breads, cheeses, and cured meats in the evening. That day we sat down to a Bulgarian meal of *kebapcheta*, which were grilled pork sausages, a *shopska* salad of tomatoes, cucumbers and feta cheese and a polenta-like dish of cornmeal and feta called *kachamak* for Stoyan. He had recently come back from a vacation home and brought me a cookbook with all his favorites in it. He spent the morning in the galley with me, directing and filling in the gaps where the rudimentary recipes left off.

"You put the onions in the pan with…" He snapped his fingers trying to make the word appear. "With cow oil." He made a stirring motion with his right arm. "And wait for it to sizzle-wizzle." It seemed his command of the English language had progressed from porn movies to children's cartoons.

Most of the crew was downstairs waiting for the Bulgarian lunch to appear. It was amazing how punctual everyone could be when food was involved; being on deck by eight in the morning was another story. I placed the platter of sausages on the table and everyone dug in.

Stoyan sat in the corner with a smile on his face from ear to ear. "Good shit." He reverted back to his stand-by.

"Thank you."

Gwen and Anna were in the laundry room with the door closed. Technically, they were in another room, but with the thin non-insulated walls they might as well have been sitting with everyone else.

"Just do it when I tell you to!" Gwen screamed in frustration.

"You sit around all day doing nothing. You do it!" Anna shot back.

The rest of the crew grew quiet. A few looked at each other knowingly. This was not the first screaming match for the two women.

"It's not my job! That's what you're here for." Gwen's tone was condescending and bordering on hysteria at the same time.

"What, to do all the work while you sit on your ass all day?" Anna's voice cut through the still air of the crew's mess.

Dylan tried to make a joke. Tom sat with his eyes down, looking at the untouched plate of food in front of him.

Patrick's jaw clenched. He ground his teeth while a small vein in his temple throbbed with his ever-quickening heartbeat. He would now have to deal with this. There was no avoiding the situation. He stood up and sighed.

I laid a hand on his arm. "They're just bored." It was the grass-is-always-greener end-of-season blues. When we had guests on board everyone dreamed of going to the shipyard to work Monday to Friday, nine to five. But once we got there and everyone had slept, they started to get fidgety and persnickety. The close proximity of your co-workers starts to grate and there's no escape. You wake up, eat, work, watch movies and go to sleep with the same nine people each and every day, with no reprieve and no privacy. Anyplace you turn there is another crewmember. No wonder crew started to fight with one another.

Chloe got up from the table. "It's okay, Patrick." She placed her plate in the dishwasher. "I'll go talk with them. It's my department."

"Thanks." Patrick looked relieved. "Let me know if you need me to step in."

If Patrick spoke with them, it would be like the boss settling an argument.

I hoped Chloe could do it in a more maternal, calm manner where all parties would feel better.

* * * *

Gwen and Anna weren't the only ones who were bored.

"What are you doing now?" I asked Patrick for the sixth time that day.

He sat at the computer entering receipts for his accounting. He sighed heavily and looked at me in frustration.

"Not now, Victoria."

"But, I'm bored, too," I complained. "Everything is clean, and I can't possibly make any more food or we'll all gain twenty pounds before the next trip."

I tried staying busy by increasing the amount of food I made, but our one small crew fridge was already bursting with Tupperware. I needed a new project.

I wandered through the boat to talk to Chloe. The rooms were quiet and empty. The girls had cleaned and sealed each room as if they were shutting down a house. Without guests, the interior of the boat felt abandoned. I found Chloe in the crew mess sewing different colored threads into everyone's uniforms.

"Can I help?"

"Are you kidding?" she asked. "I'm already stretching this job. I have enough trouble finding things for Gwen and Anna without you taking one of the few jobs left to do."

This was the strange thing about yachting. There was not enough time to do everything with guests onboard and too much time without them.

I wandered out to the deck to see if the boys needed help washing the boat. The cold winter air stung my face. A wet and dreary winter was upon us. It was a feeling I wasn't used to, because yachts usually followed the sun. This year we seemed to be hiding from it.

"No way," Dylan told me when I found him on the bow, scrub brush in hand. "I'm not having the captain's wife fall overboard on my watch."

Damn! I wasn't going to find anyone to help today. I was on my own. I returned to the galley and boiled water for tea. It was a habit I'd picked up from my friend David when I visited him in Hong Kong a few years earlier. A cup of oolong tea helped me think. As I poured steaming water over the leaves and watched them unfurl, my mind drifted back to that visit.

David and his wife Vivian spent the week touring me around every part of Hong Kong. We slurped noodle soups in crowded restaurants from one end of the city to the other. I sucked the meat off the bone of barbecued ducks and had dishes containing pig's throat and hundred-year-old eggs. We explored a different district every night as Vivian explained the history of her city and David searched for new tastes to expose me to. It was overwhelming. The lights of the city burned neon bright. The whirl of people passing, rushing to their destination, disoriented me. Vivian led the way, and I drowned in the confusion. By day three, I needed a reprieve. It was a Saturday morning and we ducked into a crowded dim sum restaurant for a meal.

"*Har gow, chiu-chao,*" a short woman with straight black hair called as she weaved her rickety cart through the labyrinth of tables. The bamboo steamers piled precariously on top jolted forward at an odd angle as the cart bumped to a stop. The oolong tea in my glass leaped up and over the edge.

Vivian said something in rapid-fire Cantonese and the woman plunked two of the steamers down in front of us.

"This one is pork." Vivian used her chopsticks to point at the dumplings nestled on a bed of cabbage. "And, this one is shrimp."

The pink of the shrimp glowed from within its translucent wrapper. I worked my chopsticks around the small bundle and prayed it wouldn't slip from my grip before I tasted what was inside. There was a luscious feel on my tongue just before the dumpling slid down my throat like a light, slippery noodle. Startled, I looked at Vivian.

"Don't worry," she said. "You'll have them again."

But, I didn't. The thing about Hong Kong is there are so many flavors and experiences to taste that you would be foolish to repeat one.

* * * *

The dumplings mystified me. I had no idea how they were made or what made the skin so see-through. I'd thought about them a lot since that day, but with guests onboard the boat I had little time to investigate what they were. Bored this day, I had a lot of time to figure them out. They could be my new project. I would learn to make the *har gow* just so I could taste them again.

My first clue at how difficult this undertaking was should have been when I bought the wheat starch from the oriental market at the top of Las Ramblas. The Chinese woman behind the counter looked at me askance. She hunched over the counter examining the package.

"What for?" she asked.

"I'm making *dim sum*," I announced proudly.

"Bah," she spat. "Just buy them. That'll be easier."

"Uh…" I stumbled.

Like a blown out fender, I slunk back to the boat deflated. I might not be able to roll dumplings like a Chinese grandmother, but I wanted to at least attempt it. How did she know they would be bad?

The next morning at eight-fifteen, I read the recipe, assembled the ingredients and began the process. I peeled the outer shell from the shrimp, minced fresh bamboo shoots to a pulp and sliced scallions. The dough felt like warm play-doh as I kneaded. I portioned and rolled the wrappers. *So far, so good.*

I picked up the first one and proceeded to rip it in half. *Oops.* Same thing happened to the second. I re-read the recipe again. It said nothing of how to avoid casualties. With the touch of an angel, I delicately picked up the third circle. Slowly, I filled it with the shrimp mixture. I pleated the edges and placed it in the steamer. I stood back and looked at my creation. It didn't look like the ones I'd eaten in Hong Kong. Maybe I should call Vivian and have her talk me through it. Mine was flat on one end with filling seeping out the other. The seam was wonky and thicker in some parts than others. The misshapen blob of dough sagged to one side. *I just need a little practice.*

"Is that lunch?" Patrick peered over my shoulder at the dumpling.

"They'll taste good," I said defensively.

"Right." He looked unconvinced.

"Aw, they're shrimp." Dylan smiled. "I can't have them."

I made a face. They were hardly being supportive. I looked at my watch. It was now past ten. I had time to perfect my technique.

For the next hour and a half, I rolled, stuffed, ripped, rerolled and steamed dumplings. It was not a pretty sight. I did improve, but only by a few degrees. At quarter to twelve I had enough oblong bundles without gaping holes to serve the crew. It took me three and a half hours to make a barely presentable meal.

I placed the platter on the table. The crew looked dubious.

"Not good," Stoyan shook his head. He reached into the fridge and grabbed the *kebapcheta* from the day before.

Chloe was the first to try. She dipped the slippery dumpling into the sweet soy and popped it in her mouth. She had the same startled look I had upon first bite.

"They're delicious!" She said. "Are you going to make these for the guests?"

"Bah!" I mimicked the little old lady at the grocery. "I'll just buy them. That'll be easier."

Kebapcheta (Bulgarian Sausages) and Shopska Salad

1 pound ground pork
1 pound ground beef
2 tablespoons Greek yogurt
1 onion, minced
3 tablespoons chopped parsley
1-1/2 teaspoons sea salt
1 teaspoon cumin
1 teaspoon savory
18 grinds black pepper
2 egg whites

Combine all in a mixing bowl. Test a piece by heating a small skillet over medium-high heat. Pinch off a tablespoon of meat and form a small patty. Sear in the pan 2 minutes each side. Cool and taste for seasoning. *Must be highly seasoned.

Let the mixture sit in the fridge for 2 hours to marry the flavors.
Wet your hands and form mixture into 4-inch cylindrical sausages.
Grill on medium-high heat for 5 minutes until cooked through.
Serve with shopska salad

Shopska Salad:
4 green onions, sliced
4 tomatoes, chopped in 1-inch cubes
1 cucumber, peeled, quartered lengthwise and chopped in $\frac{1}{2}$" slices
1 green pepper, sliced in thin strips
1 red pepper, sliced in thin strips
1/4 cup parsley, chopped
1 teaspoon sea salt
18 grinds black pepper
2 tablespoons red wine vinegar
1/4 cup olive oil
24 kalamata olives, pitted and sliced in half
1 cup feta cheese, grated

Combine spring onions, tomatoes, cucumbers, peppers, parsley, sea salt, black pepper, red wine vinegar and olive oil. Place in salad bowls and garnish with kalamata olives and grated feta cheese.

Serves 8

Har Gow

When I first attempted this recipe, I thought it was too much work. But after the first trial, I realized they were easy, just delicate, but definitely worth the time. I set aside three hours and make enough to freeze for future use. These are tasty afternoon snacks, hors d'oerves, or light lunches.

Sweet Soy Dipping Sauce:
1/4 cup soy sauce
2 tablespoons rice wine vinegar
2 tablespoons water
1 teaspoon brown sugar
1 teaspoon toasted sesame oil

Whisk all together and set aside.

Shrimp Filling:
1 pound shrimp, peeled and chopped into $\frac{1}{4}$" dice.
3/4 teaspoon sea salt
2 tablespoons fatty bacon, minced
3 tablespoons bamboo shoots, rinsed and chopped fine
1 tablespoon green onions, white part only, diced fine
1-1/2 teaspoons cornstarch
3/4 teaspoon sugar
1/8 teaspoon white pepper
1-1/2 teaspoons Shaoxing rice wine
1 teaspoon sesame oil

Mix together diced bacon, bamboo shoots and green onions and mince finely with a knife until well combined. Mix into shrimp and set aside. In a smaller bowl, whisk together cornstarch, sugar, white pepper, Shaoxing rice wine, and sesame oil. Mix into the shrimp and marinate for 30 minutes while you mix the dough.

Wheat Starch Dough:
1 cup wheat starch
1/2 cup tapioca starch
1/4 teaspoon sea salt
1 cup boiled water, cooled for 2 minutes
4 teaspoons canola oil

~Continued on next page

Mix wheat starch, tapioca starch and salt. Pour in half the hot water and stir with a wooden spoon until incorporated. Add the rest of the hot water and work into dough. Add canola oil as soon as dough begins to come together and knead with your hands for a minute to make a smooth, play-doh like dough. Divide into four equal balls and cover with plastic wrap. Rest for 5 minutes before rolling.

Slice a Ziplock bag down the sides and brush with canola oil. Roll one of the portions of dough into a one-inch log and divide into 8 portions. Cover with plastic wrap. Take one portion, roll it into a ball and press between the Ziplock bag with a flat-bottomed glass to create a four-inch thin circle. Set aside and cover with plastic wrap. Repeat process with all eight small pieces.

Making the dumplings:

Place one of the rounds in your slightly cupped hand, gently. Spoon two teaspoons of filling into the center. Gently close your hand around the filling to seal the edges of the dough in a half moon. Place in a bamboo steamer basket lined with baking paper. Repeat with the rest of the circles. Use a little canola oil on your fingertips and gently crimp the edges of each parcel to make a decorative wave pattern.

Place steamer over boiling water. Cover and steam for six minutes.

Repeat procedure with the next disk of dough while the dumplings are steaming.

Remove finished dumplings and place on a plate to serve with sweet soy dipping sauce. Or, cool and refrigerate for up to two days or freeze for up to one month. Re-steam for 3 minutes to heat.

Makes 16

The Call

Another month went by where we all squeezed our brains thinking of jobs to do. The boat looked fabulous, and we were more organized for the upcoming season than I had ever been on any previous vessel. I just wished we knew when and where our new season would be. The phone remained painfully silent, with no news from the manager.

Our days filled and rolled over as the sun began to shine through the rain clouds for longer periods each day. Small, fragrant buds of spring painted the canvas of Barcelona almost overnight. The beach filled with people trying to soak in as much warmth as possible. Patios were crowded with patrons. The city came out of hibernation.

I was in the galley chopping vegetables for a salad when Patrick came in. He bit the side of his lip. "The owner just called me."

I was taken aback. "The owner?" We hadn't heard anything from him since we first took the job. All our information came through the manager.

"Yeah, he wants me to fly to New York next week to meet with him."

"Maybe he'll give you some answers for this season's plan."

The corners of Patrick's mouth curled skyward. "He already did."

I raised my hands and shrugged in question. "Well? What are we doing? Where are we headed?"

Patrick's smile became mischievous. "How do you feel about going on a world cruise?"

My head spun fast. I dropped the knife I was holding. "What?" I sputtered.

Patrick laughed. "The owner liked how we handled all the charters this year and would like to branch out, see more of the world." Patrick grabbed my hand. "He wants us to leave for Malaysia next month."

"Are you serious?" I asked in disbelief.

Patrick nodded. "Then through Indonesia, down to Australia, New Zealand and up through Fiji, Tahiti, Micronesia, Palau, the Philippines, China…" Patrick ticked off place names on his fingers. "He also mentioned Thailand, Vietnam, and Japan."

All the places I had been dreaming about were being laid out in front of me like a menu. My eyes glazed with excitement. I began bouncing on the balls of my feet as the exotic names continued.

"Can we do all that?" I asked. Not believing what I was hearing.

A sparkle entered Patrick's eye. He grabbed my shaking hands. "Yeah. Why not?" He shrugged his shoulders and smiled. "What could go wrong?"

Culinary Glossary

Baklava- a layered sweet pastry made of phyllo, chopped nuts and honey

Bellini- a Venitian cocktail of Prosecco and white peach puree

Bolognese- a meat-based sauce for pasta from Bologna, Italy

Boulangerie- French bakery and bread shop

Bresaola- Italian air-dried beef

Cacik- Turkish yogurt sauce

Caponata- a Sicilian cooked vegetable stew

Chiu-chao- Chinese steamed pork dumplings

Dim Sum- various Chinese dishes, typically served as a series of small dishes

Enchiladas- Mexican corn tortillas rolled around a filling, sauced and baked

Florina Peppers- a variety of Greek long red peppers

Focaccia- flat Italian bread

Haloumi- Greek hard cheese made from goat and sheep milk, often seared in a pan

Har Gow- Chinese steamed shrimp dumplings

Iberico Ham- Spanish ham made from pigs that graze on acorns

Kachamak- a Bulgarian polenta-like cornmeal dish served with grated feta cheese

Kebapcheta- Bulgarian grilled sausages

Kung Pao- classic Sichuan dish of deep-fried chicken and peppers

Manchego Cheese- Spanish sheep's milk hard cheese

Marcona Almonds- Spanish variety of almond typically sold deep-fried and salted

Mojo- a Cuban citrus-spice marinade

Moussaka- a layered eggplant and ground lamb lasagna-type dish

Porchetta- an Italian pork roast

Queso Fresca- Mexican fresh cheese

Ras-al-Hanout- Moroccan curry powder of 37 different spices

Ratatouille- Provençal vegetable stew

Shopska- Bulgarian tomato, cucumber and feta cheese salad

Sis Kabab- Turkish lamb skewers

Snezhanka- Bulgarian yogurt sauce

Tortilla- Spanish potato and egg omelet

Tsatziki- Greek yogurt sauce

Vongoli- Italian pasta dish with clam sauce

About the Author

Victoria Allman has been following her stomach around the globe for twelve years as a yacht chef. She writes about her floating culinary odyssey through Europe, the Caribbean, Nepal, Vietnam, Africa, and the South Pacific in her first book, *Sea Fare: A Chef's Journey Across the Ocean.*

Victoria is a columnist for *Dockwalk*, an International magazine for crew members aboard yachts. Her column "Dishing It Up" is a humorous look at cooking for the rich and famous in an ever-moving galley.

A chapter from *Sea Fare* was reprinted in the anthology *Female Nomad and Friends* by Rita Golden Gelman.

She also regularly contributes tales of her tasty adventures to *Marina Life Magazine* and *OceanLines.*

In 2010, Victoria received a Royal Palm Literary Award from the Florida Writers Association. You can read more of her food-driven escapades through her web-site, www.victoriaallman.com

Acknowledgements

As always, my family has been more supportive than I could imagine, and even though I'm sure they think it, they've never questioned the choice I made to dive head first into this crazy world called yachting. Thank you Mom, Paul, Nancy, Jeff, Mara, Ella and Dad.

I am indebted to my Thursday night writers group who taught me how to tell a story and who strengthened my writing. Many of these stories made their debut in Dockwalk magazine. Thank you to the group of editors and friends in both places who have encouraged me to keep writing and telling funny stories.

Many stories would never have come to light without my friends and crewmembers who rode the seas with me. Thank you for making me laugh in the first place.

My appreciation goes out to Dan Brooks who makes me smile each time I see his graphic creation of Chef Victoria on these pages.

Thanks to my agent, Sammie Justesen, who believed in my writing from day one and saw it through rough waters to the smooth sailing at NorLightsPress, with publishers Dee Justesen and Nadene Carter.

And, to my main character on the page and in my heart, Patrick. Thank you for giving me a life and love to write about.

.

Available from NorlightsPress and
fine booksellers everywhere

Toll free: 888-558-4354   **Online:** www.norlightspress.com
Shipping Info: Add $2.95 for first item and $1.00 for each additional item

Name _____

Address _____

Daytime Phone _____

E-mail _____

No. Copies	Title	Price (each)	Total Cost
	Subtotal		
	Shipping		
	Total		

Payment by (circle one):

   Check   Visa   Mastercard   Discover   Am Express

Card number_____3 digit code_____

Exp.date_____ Signature_____

Mailing Address:
2323 S.R. 252
Martinsville, IN 46151

Sign up to receive our catalogue at
www.norlightspress.com

CPSIA information can be obtained at www.ICGtesting.com
Printed in the USA
LVOW091421290712

292026LV00003B/8/P

9 781935 254379